Break Free of Parenting Pressures

Embrace Your Natural Guidance

Debbie Pokornik, BA, BSW

iUniverse, Inc.
New York Bloomington

iUniverse books may be ordered through booksellers or by contacting:

iUniverse
1663 Liberty Drive
Bloomington, IN 47403
www.iuniverse.com
1-800-Authors (1-800-288-4677)

ISBN: 978-1-4502-1010-2 (sc)
ISBN: 978-1-4502-1011-9 (ebook)
ISBN: 978-1-4502-1009-6 (dj)

Printed in the United States of America

iUniverse rev. date: 04/09/2010

Artwork by Teresa D. Shepit
Imagine Illustration and Graphic Design
t@imagineu.ca

For Dani, Wilem, and Alissa

Contents

Preface... xi

Acknowledgments.. xiii

Introduction...xv

    The Book... xvii

    My Anonymous Message..................................... xix

Part 1 Being a Parent

Chapter 1: The Perfect Parent...**3**

    My Guilt Trip 3

    Parenting Is Tough 4

    Our Parenting Dream 8

    What Is Our Job? 9

    Exercise: You Are Here ∇ 16

Chapter 2: Believe It or Not...**20**

    My Inheritance 20

    What Are We Really Up Against?...........................21

    As a Matter of Belief ... I Do! 25

    Exercise: What Do You Believe?............................28

Chapter 3: This Is Your Body Speaking..............................**32**

    My Lesson in Fear 32

    The "F" Word..33

    Tuning In to Our Signals.......................................36

    Exercise: Taking Charge of Your Body.................41

Chapter 4: Getting Back on Course **44**

    My Moment of Clarity 44

    What's the Big Idea?...45

    Strategies That Help Us Focus on the Big Idea 47

    Finding Our Way...48

Building Relationships..49

Counting on Success...52

Exercise: Setting Life Priorities...........................53

Part 2 Understanding You and Your Family

Chapter 5: Where Did *That* Come From?..............57

My Tween Adjustment..57

What We Don't Know Can Hurt Us 59

It Runs in the Family..60

Creating a Balanced Family...............................62

Let's Get Personal 63

From Learning to Love 70

Exercise: Creating the Family You Want..........76

Chapter 6: A Powerful Topic..................................80

My Bathtime Trials 80

Understanding Our Response-Ability................82

Response-Ability Lies within Us.......................85

Introducing Parent Power 87

A Force *Not* to Be Reckoned With...................90

Surviving a Power Struggle 96

Now That You're Calm, Let's Deal with the Storm..........97

Exercise: The Game of Blame 100

Chapter 7: Creating Structure and Control............103

My Clothing Concerns......................................103

Practicing Self-Control 104

Regaining Control in the Heat of the Moment.............108

Creating Structure 110

Bullying: A Dishonorable Mention..................117

Exercise: Making the Rules 119

Part 3 A FREE Parenting Pack

Chapter 8: Packing With Care **127**

My Calling Plan 127

Our Hidden Baggage..130

Unloading the Heavy Stuff 132

Replacing Our Heavy Tools..134

Knowing How to Pack 137

Strategies That Build...140

Exercise: What Are You Packing? 146

Chapter 9: Making Common Strategies FREE **151**

My Power Play..151

For Every Action 153

Stop, or That Privilege Is Gone......................................158

You Are So Grounded 161

Penalty Called ... Time-Out..164

Exercise: Clear Expectations 171

Chapter 10: Working Through Problems..........................**174**

My Learning Chart...174

What's the Problem?..176

The Captured Toy Box..180

The Battle for Bedtime 187

Taking Tantrums off the Menu..191

Exercise: Creating a Good IDEA.....................................195

Chapter 11: Are We Communicating? **198**

My Do-Over Option...198

What Did You Call Me?..201

Connecting through Conversation 204

Communicating Our Underlying Message 207

Keeping Communication Flowing....................................211

Stand Up and Be Counted...214

Exercise: Being a Good Listener 218

Part 4 Caring for the Caregiver

Chapter 12: Controlling Our Personal Pressure.....................223

My Time-Out Penalty 223

Be the Elastic 225

Little Things, Big Stress—A Look at Childcare 231

Your Number-One Fan.......................................234

Exercise: Bag It All!..237

Chapter 13: Keeping a Healthy Perspective...........................240

My Extracurricular Challenge 240

What Do We Need?...244

Putting Our Needs First 247

Where Does All Our Time Go?........................251

Exercise: Creating Your Picture.......................252

Conclusion **257**

Embracing Change..257

Breaking Free...259

Bibliography **261**

Resources **263**

Further Reading 263

Web Sites...264

Preface

My husband and I decided to start our family fifteen years ago, when I was going to university. Since I was attending the Faculty of Social Work, the news that I was pregnant sparked a lot of interesting conversations. My fellow students wanted to debate topics like spanking, family beds, feeding on demand, and any other controversial parenting issues that came to mind. I had no idea at that time what kind of parent I was going to be, but I dreamt of being a great one. I quickly realized that turning this dream into reality was going to require more strategies and knowledge than I currently had, so I began learning everything I could on the topic.

I was surprised at how hard it was to adopt new parenting tools and what a large role personal development played in effective parenting. I thought I would be much better at being consistent and knowing what to do when things went wrong. I was shocked by the intensity of my emotions around my children and the pressure to "do the right thing" when I didn't always know what the right thing was. The desire to be perfect was there, the knowledge and support to help me do that was not.

Today, I am still not a perfect parent although I have accepted this as normal and, in fact, preferable. I have become knowledgeable on social and emotional development and have learned and created a lot of great parenting strategies. My children (I have two teenagers now) are regular kids who challenge me often, providing ample opportunity to practice my skills.

My desire to learn, practice, and share with others led me quite naturally into the role of parent educator. Working as a prevention social worker with a local school division provided me with plenty of opportunity to work with parents, teachers, students, and others on many areas of social and emotional skill development. I have led many parenting seminars and been trained in many great programs.

What I've learned is that, as different as we all are, most of us will benefit from some support, understanding, and helpful suggestions at some point in our journey, especially in the area of parenting. The more I learn, the more passionate I become about providing support to all parents in whatever area they feel they could use it the most. Writing this book seemed like a good way to do that. We are all doing the best we can with what we know. Let's look at what we know and build on it in whatever way feels right.

Acknowledgments

Thank you to Beverley Doern, Dani Pokornik, and Rhonda Taylor for finding the time and patience to read through my book at its early stages. Thank you to Teresa Shepit for being my longtime friend and taking time out of her busy schedule to provide illustrations and cover ideas for this book. Thank you to Lesley Eblie for believing in my ability as a writer and parent educator and encouraging me to go beyond our school newsletters.

Thank you to my kids, Wilem and Alissa, for providing me with so much love and encouragement while still keeping me on track as a parent. You are wonderful kids to learn with, and I thank you for bringing so much joy into my life. Thank you to my best friend and partner in life, Dani, who believes in me despite my quirky nature. Your solid support and love means more than I can tell you. Finally, thank you to my parents, Bob and Elaine Gregg, who taught me the meaning of perspicacity and instilled in me an unwavering connection to family. You guys are awesome, and I love you!

Introduction

This book has been written for parents who are struggling at their role of parenting and need ideas they can use right away to bring things around; parents who are not struggling but want ideas for building strong, positive connections with their kids; and parents who have made it their mission to be the best they can be and raise kids who will thrive regardless of life circumstances.

The information is relevant regardless of skin colour, financial situation, family makeup, or sexual orientation. The skills and understandings that are important for parenting are based on universal human requirements that do not change with circumstance. It is the *how* of parenting that makes a difference more than the *what*.

As unique as we all are, the pieces of parenting that will most influence our success in raising resilient children are the same. We all have different starting points and dynamics in our homes that will influence how challenging it is for us to focus on this task, but the basic information never changes.

No matter what your situation, you have what it takes to make a difference in your child's life. Yes, it will be more challenging if you do not have the resources available or are lacking the support and assistance of others. I would love to be able to provide each parent with the perfect solution to their every need, but this is not realistic. I find parents know their situation better than any outside "expert" and often do a much better job of adapting parenting strategies to make them work for their family. As a result, I've provided a variety of ideas and suggestions throughout the book, with the hope that you will feel inspired to take those that fit your circumstance and adapt them to meet your needs.

If your children are teenagers and you are just starting to make changes, some of the tasks I discuss will be harder to do. You will be best served to focus your energy on the relationship building ideas and only correct your child's behaviour when absolutely necessary. If mutual respect has not been built by this stage, kids tend to rebel with delight, so focus on building respect and your own personal growth, if you really want to see a difference.

Safety concerns and unhealthy living conditions will add extra stress and worry for parents. I hope it's comforting to know that the aspects of parenting that help kids grow into balanced resilient human beings are centered more on love, acceptance, belonging, and understanding than anything else. Regardless of your socioeconomic background, maturity level, or access to resources, you have what it takes to do this task.

As a social worker, parent educator, and parent, I have spent the last fifteen years learning why parenting is so challenging and how I can help people feel good about their role as parents. I have been accredited in programs like Triple P, Positive Parenting Program from Australia, and have created several programs of my own. I have learned that parenting brings with it emotional upsets that cannot be anticipated no matter how forward-thinking we might be.

The goal of this book is to provide quick helpful ideas, validations, and reminders to make parenting less stressful and to help remove some of the self-doubt and uncertainty most parents experience. It is meant to give you a laugh, help you feel good about your parenting role, and empower you to embrace your natural guidance.

The chapters have been supplemented with exercises, personal stories, thought-provoking articles, and suggested resources so enthusiastic readers can use this book to guide them toward major changes. I've also included **f**un, **r**ealistic, **e**asy and **e**ffective tips, which I call *FREE Parenting tips,* for those who prefer the ideas without any explanation at all.

You know your family and your situation better than anyone else. Use this book for ideas and support, but always remember that you are the expert in your home. In the end, it is you who has to feel good about any changes you decide to make.

I believe every parent starts out wanting to do the best job she can and believing she has what it takes to reach this goal. My job is to help you reconnect with that knowledge.

The Book

Part 1 is meant to remind us why we became a parent in the first place. It focuses on the big idea and challenges us to think about what this job really entails.

Part 2 focuses on understanding what makes humans tick. When we are aware of the traits that make our family unique, it is easier for us to have realistic expectations. The more we know and understand about ourselves, the easier it is to build relationships and feel good about the people in our lives.

Part 3 spotlights our parenting pack, the tools and strategies we use to teach our kids right from wrong and maintain our sanity in the process. It uses the FREE acronym as a guideline for taking common parenting ideas and adjusting them to do what we need them to do.

Part 4 provides a quick peek at things you might do to make your life less stressful and more balanced. It's about making sure you are being your own number-one fan so that you have the endurance and enthusiasm to make things happen in every area of your life. Kids learn more from what we do than from what we say. We need to model self-care if we want them to get it.

It is natural for people to allow life to flow when things are going well and only make changes when absolutely necessary. If we want to be proactive, we can't wait until things go wrong to act. We need to do some work in those good moments to build a strong family foundation so that when the tough times arise, we come through it okay.

Breaking free of parenting pressures is about taking back our power as parents and embracing our natural guidance. We are all perfectly qualified to do this job, and the sooner we believe it the better.

My Anonymous Message

When I remind people they should pay attention to how they talk to their kids and make it a habit to use a nice voice, they look at me like I'm pointing out the obvious. Most of us believe we are nice most of the time and would be shocked or disappointed to hear otherwise. I was one of these people until the day when the universe conspired to show me differently.

On this fateful day, my kids and I were hurrying off to an appointment that we were already late for. I was rushing my kids, trying to get them to pick up the pace, and the more I pushed the more they resisted. Finally, I got them buckled into their car seats and started off to my destination. At that point, I should have been able to relax. The drive was going to take us forty-five minutes no matter which route I took and I'd arrive at my appointment only a couple of minutes late.

Here's the amazing part: Somehow, in the struggle to get my kids into the car, I had managed to push a button on my cell phone and call my house. I have no idea how that happened and knew nothing about it until I returned home and retrieved the message.

There, on my machine, was this evil woman talking to these little kids in an angry, condescending voice. It took me a few moments to even recognize that the voice I was hearing was my own. What shocked me most wasn't what I was saying, it was the voice I was using and the terse way I was saying things.

I heard my sweet little four-year-old ask me to turn on the music. My sharp voice responded, "No, we don't need music right now! I just need some peace and quiet!" My son started to complain, and I responded immediately with little accusations of how he had made me late and how much I hated being late.

I was not being nice and would not have believed it if I hadn't heard it myself. This was definitely not how I like to think I talk to anyone, especially the two most precious people in my life. It was an eye-opener and has resulted in my paying attention to the voice I'm using and altering it when it isn't reflecting the kind of person I believe myself to be.

I've never managed to accidentally phone home again, but I took that little lesson to heart and believe I'm a better mom because of it.

Part 1

Being a Parent

Chapter 1: The Perfect Parent

My Guilt Trip

Guilt is an interesting weight we put on our own shoulders and then carry around as if it's a cross we have to bear. When my son was about four years old, he was bouncing a ball around my home office. I think I asked to him to stop, but because I was so focused on work, I'm not totally sure. His ball (which was a hard little super bouncer) hit the tile in our entranceway and bounced up to set the hanging light swinging before shooting across my desk and onto the floor. That got my attention!

I jumped up, turned to my son, and yelled, "I told you to stop. You almost broke the light, you knocked papers off my desk, and you nearly hit me! Give me your ball—it's gone for the afternoon."

My son started to cry at the same time the doorbell rang. It was a deliveryman from a nearby town, and my cheeks burned as I realized he had heard the whole exchange. I could barely talk or meet the man's eye.

You might be wondering about my strong reaction to someone overhearing me yelling. So let me remind you that I am a parent educator. I am not supposed to yell—I am supposed to be controlled and in charge of any and every parenting situation life throws my way. At least that's what I believed back then.

For the rest of the day, I replayed the scene in my mind wondering at my loss of temper, my lack of parenting skills, and my total hypocrisy at calling myself an educator. I wondered how my son could get over my loss of control in less than an hour while I struggled with it for the rest of the day.

Later, confessing my guilt to a friend, she sighed deeply in frustration. "At what point are you going to stop beating yourself up? You made a mistake," she said. "You're a great mom and a great parent educator. Your son accepted your apology, why can't you?"

Why not, indeed? I like to tell people, you can't send someone on a guilt trip unless their bags are already packed. I guess my bags were packed and ready to go.

Parenting Is Tough

Becoming a parent is one of the most natural things we do, yet it is also one of the hardest. What other job requires us to be on duty twenty-four hours a day, seven days a week, three hundred and sixty-five days a year? A friend of mine, who is a stay-at-home mother, joked, "I have the kind of job that if I miss a day, I go to jail." This might seem exaggerated, and those of us who work outside of the home might find it questionable, but the point is well taken: being a parent is serious business.

Having said that, I'm not sure the demanding hours are what make this job so tough. What seems to wear us down is the amount of emotion that is wrapped up in being a parent and all the stresses and concerns that go with it. When our kids are young, all they have to do is shed a few tears or cling to our legs when we try to leave and their hooks are sunk painfully into our hearts. Having a verbal war with them minutes before they leave for school can finish us for the day. They head out the door and often forget a conversation even took place, while we carry it around sharing it with others and wondering if our child will be damaged for life. I've seen some very powerful and respected people in the workplace turn to mush after having it out with their child.

The truth is most of us would rather cut off our arm than see our child go through a painful experience. If our child is threatened, we immediately fall into the mother bear role (even fathers can do this) and are ready to mow down anyone or anything we see as threatening to our cub. There's not a lot of thought that goes into that response: it's pure, unfettered emotion.

As if that's not enough, our society is very judgmental of parents. They point fingers at us if we don't control our kids to their satisfaction. They tell us to lighten up if we appear to control them too much. With eyebrows raised, they watch what we ingest during pregnancy and blame us for our breastfeeding infant's gassy discomfort. They insist we read to our children daily and spend precious evening hours helping them with homework we don't even understand. Our car seats, cribs, and highchairs must all fit current guidelines, and we should never let our baby sleep with us … or is it without us?

While some of these concerns are valid and given with positive intentions, we, the parents, can end up feeling judged and criticized no matter what we do. If we don't perform well, there is the fear our child will be removed from our home. If we do too much, there is the fear our child will never leave our home.

If parenting is one of the most natural things we do, why is it so challenging? Perhaps we bring it on ourselves. Despite having no formal training, we seem to feel that we should know all the answers and be perfect at every aspect of its delivery. We allow others to judge us and make us think we need to do things, or avoid things, that we know feel wrong and will regret later.

> *FREE Parenting Tip: We are our own worst critics and often make parenting tougher than it needs to be. Allowing others to judge us and make us feel like we are not measuring up is a choice. Believe in yourself! You are a work in progress and absolutely perfect for the job of being you!*

As parents, we need to stand united and support one another. We need to feel comfortable asking for help with this challenging, sometimes heart-wrenching, task and acknowledge that every one of us can use support at some point in the parenting experience.

Above all, we need to remember that kids are extremely resilient and forgiving. We will not "ruin" them every time we make a mistake. We teach them to be strong and forgiving when we practice being those things ourselves. Parenting, and the many opportunities it provides to make mistakes, allows us ample opportunity to model how to do this for our kids.

People can be sent on a guilt trip only if their bags are already packed. In other words, if we believe we should know everything and be perfect at being a parent, we create guilt every time we make a mistake.

On the other hand, if we allow ourselves to admit we don't have all the answers, some of the pressure will disappear. With that weight removed from our shoulders, perhaps we can allow ourselves to really enjoy the incredible journey we have embarked upon.

Follow the Leader

My definition of a good leader is someone who inspires others to do their best by focusing on being the best he or she can be. In other words, the best way to get our kids to work with us is to focus on ourselves first. Ask yourself the following questions:

- Am I acting in a way I would like my child to imitate, or am I telling him one thing and modeling another?

- Am I enjoying most of my days by focusing on the positives, or am I pointing out all the things that went wrong and all the problems I have encountered?

- Am I building myself up on a regular basis, believing in my own ability and taking pride in the things I have accomplished; or am I downplaying the goals I reach and belittling my efforts?

There is no skill involved in bossing people around; there is a lot of skill involved in being a good boss. If we want to be a leader in our family, we must focus first on the one thing within our control—ourselves.

When we focus on being positive, giving others the benefit of the doubt, forgiving mistakes, and controlling our emotions, we feel good about ourselves. We are also inspiring these qualities in our kids.

Our Parenting Dream

We begin to envision the type of person we'd like to become from a young age. We watch others around us, develop ideas about what works or doesn't, and begin modeling ourselves in that image. The feedback we get from other people, along with our own assessment, will accelerate our growth, make it harder for us to achieve, or cause us to change the course we had originally set out on.

When we behave in a way that fits with this image, we feel a wonderful sense of *rightness*. When we fail to measure up to our created image, we feel anxious, frustrated, or disappointed. Often, if we feel we are not measuring up to our mental picture, our sense of self-worth becomes damaged, making it hard for us to reach our full potential.

This is important because if we remember the mental picture we created when we found out a baby was on its way, it can help us understand why we often have conflicting feelings as we parent. Typically, our picture included lots of loving, caring moments where we consoled and cuddled with our child. We knew how to help him when he was hurting and he confided in us on a regular basis. We avoided many of the errors our caregivers made and came up with new creative ways to work through any challenging situations.

In other words, we were really great parents in our dream and our child loved us unconditionally as a result. Perhaps this distortion of reality is a protective mechanism. If we pictured all the challenging moments first, we might back out and procreation would become a thing of the past!

One of the problems with our generated picture is that we control how other people behave in our dreamy situations. Our child is rarely cranky or rude. Our partner doesn't lose his cool. Our parenting knowledge is abundant. This dream is within our control, but reality is not. The only person we truly have control over is ourselves, and without all the "real-life stressors" we behave perfectly.

It is in our best interest to identify what changes are required to get us back on course and focus on making it happen. Writing the dream off as unrealistic or too hard won't change our uncomfortable feelings. Only working toward matching our dream behaviour to our current behaviour will do.

Being a good parent means doing the best we can with what we have and being open to learning more. Staying aware of the kind of parent we originally envisioned and the kind of relationship we are hoping to build with our kids is very important. It might require some support and being open to help, but it's well worth it. When we align our behaviour and our thoughts with our dreams and aspirations, the sky is the limit. Right now, our kids are envisioning the kind of person they want to be when they grow up; let's help them create a good one.

> *FREE Parenting Tip: Become aware of the kind of parent you originally thought that you would be and notice how it aligns with the kind of parent you are today. The more these two line up with each other, the better you will feel.*

What Is Our Job?

When parents are asked to create a job description for their parenting role, they typically list things like the following:

- Provide for our children (keep them safe, fed, etc.)
- Teach them right from wrong in a way that makes them want to do the right thing (help them learn from their mistakes)
- Love our kids and help them feel good about who they are as people
- Provide opportunities for our kids to try new things

Rarely do parents believe their job is to do the following:

- Make their kids happy
- Save their kids from pain or predictable mistakes
- Impress other adults
- Control their child's behaviour

Yet this second list is what often comes up when parents start talking about the things that are causing them concern. Let's address these beliefs first.

"I really just want her to be happy."
"Unless I'm playing with him, he's bored."
"Sometimes I give in to make her happy."

When parents make these comments, they are talking about their child's happiness as if it is their job to satisfy this need. It is beneficial to provide kids with an emotionally stable environment to grow up in. When people feel loved, understood, accepted, and safe, it is easier for them to be happy. But this is different from actually "making" someone feel a certain way.

True happiness comes from within, and we can drive ourselves crazy if we believe we must create that feeling in another. We can help to make our kids' environment fun, engaging, and loving, but we cannot guarantee how they will feel. A child can be bored at Disney World and happy at the dentist's office; we cannot control that. If we could, wouldn't we use that power for much greater things?

"I lived that when I was young, and I don't want that to happen to her."

"I remember what those parties were like. There's no way he's going to them."

"I just don't want him to fail—I remember how that hurt for me."

Life is full of contrast, which results in pain or discomfort. This contrast makes us wish for something better and then grow toward that wish. Pain is an important motivator that pushes us to grow. Although we might want to eliminate pain from our child's life, it is impossible to do so and works against our desire to raise strong, resilient kids. Providing a safe environment is different from eliminating pain and discomfort.

Mistakes are something we often have to live through to appreciate. Although others can share their experiences with us, their lessons do not affect us the same way and therefore do not result in the same type of learning. It is hard for us as parents to clearly see a mistake our child is about to make and still allow her freedom to move in that direction. This is exactly what needs to happen, however, and, no matter how much we interfere, she will continue finding ways to create that experience. In the end, it is our relationship with her that suffers despite our best intentions.

"Everyone was watching. I was so embarrassed."

"I'm sure the other parents were shocked that I couldn't stop
   him."
"I know the other moms were wishing I hadn't brought her to
   the playgroup"

None of us like to think others are judging and finding us lacking.
When a teacher calls home, when our child is benched at a game, when
people look annoyed because our child is too loud, we feel the pressure
and react accordingly. Even when no one else is around, our thoughts
will often focus on how other people would react if they knew what
just happened.

The truth is that no matter how good we are at something, there
will always be people who refuse to be impressed by our abilities. In the
end, those other people really don't matter. We need to let go of what
other people think and put our energy where it counts, which is into
being the parent we really want to be.

"If I could just make her listen …"
"He never does what I say! I must be doing it wrong."
"I told her not to, but she did it anyway. I'm wasting my
   breath."

Hand in hand with the idea of impressing other adults is the notion
that we should be able to control our children. This influences our
behaviour as parents because it makes us think child control is within
our ability. True and total control will always be beyond our grasp.
Remembering that helps us think more creatively.

So what is our job? The most obvious part of our job as parents is
providing for our children's basic needs. Our kids need things like food,

sleep, shelter, and safety. If we cannot provide it, they will have trouble focusing on personal growth and achievement. This does not mean they will not succeed in life; it does mean these things will demand their attention before anything else. For example, if a child is starving, he will struggle to learn at school and might steal even though he knows it's dangerous or wrong.

The second part of our job is to meet the social and emotional needs of our child. Emotional needs involve loving our kids and helping them feel worthy. It includes things like unconditional love, acceptance, trust, self-worth, and understanding. If we do not provide this for our children, they will seek it elsewhere as soon as they are able. This can result in gang membership, sexual promiscuity, or other challenges many of us would prefer to avoid.

> *FREE Parenting Tip: Our most important task as parents is to ensure our kids feel loved, accepted, appreciated, and understood. If we focus on their social and emotional needs by working on our own gaps, we will both (all) flourish.*

A child whose basic needs are not always met can still thrive when emotional needs are looked after. On the other hand, a child whose basic needs are met but whose emotional needs are not, can struggle for a lifetime.

Social needs involve things like getting along with others, empathizing, being compassionate, assertive and practicing self-control. They help us function successfully in our world and allow us to build positive relationships. A person with gaps in these areas can suffer as she tries to move forward in relationships with friends, colleagues, and life partners. The more we can provide for those needs, the more she will grow as a person and build connections with others.

Meeting these needs is not always easy, especially when most of us are not skilled in them ourselves. The trick is to meet the needs you can meet and then put your energy into your own growth in these areas. When you do this, you will naturally model the skills you are trying to teach and everyone will benefit.

That's it. Our job is to satisfy these three areas of need. If we do so, our children will naturally strive to learn and grow. They will look up to us and seek our guidance as life provides them with challenges to learn from, and we can rest assured we are doing our job.

Parenting Job Description

Knowing what we are trying to achieve in our role as parents makes it easier for us to be good at our job. Here's a sample job description of this much-sought-after role.

Your job, should you choose to accept it, is to do the following:

- Provide your children with structure and boundaries within which they can safely grow to their full potential
- Guide your children toward appropriate behaviour by teaching them *how* to think for themselves
- Provide your kids with opportunities to grow, try, make mistakes and learn
- Teach your kids respect by treating them respectfully and earning (rather than insisting on) their respect
- Be a positive role model especially when it comes to self-discipline, emotional control, and problem solving

- Let your kids know they are loved unconditionally, that they are very important to you, that you will always believe in them and will have their back when they are in need of support
- Other duties as required

Qualities all applicants will benefit from are the following:

- Patience and open-mindedness
- Ability to laugh at ridiculous and often embarrassing moments
- Ability to be a team player
- Willingness to learn and adapt
- Ability to be a self-starter
- Ability to work well under pressure
- Ability to be clear about expectations/beliefs
- Willingness to share with others
- Creativity
- A loving attitude
- Excellent self-control in times of high stress and button-pushing situations
- Ability to forgive self and others for inappropriate behaviour

All individuals welcome to apply; accidental applications accepted!

Exercise: You Are Here ∇

It's hard to get where you are going if you don't know where you are starting from. This exercise will help you get a picture of where you are today so that you can begin to plan where you would like to go in the future.

1. Think about the mental picture you created when you found out you were going to be a parent. Write down a few of the key things that describe the parent you planned on being in the beginning. Sometimes it helps to think about the things you valued most (or swore to change) from your own upbringing and use some of them to get you going.

    Examples:

    I spend quality time with my child and laugh with him a lot. My daughter and I can talk about anything. She trusts me and values my opinion. I tuck my kids in nightly, complete with bedtime story, hugs and giggles.

    My kids feel safe and loved, they can come to me for anything.

    I am ...patient, a good listener, approachable, supportive, funny.

    _____

    _____

    _____

    _____

    _____

    _____

2. On a scale of one to ten (with ten being *definitely agree*), decide how well you are living up to the various aspects of the picture

of yourself you just described. You may go back and measure each statement if you like, and then give yourself an overall rating here. Overall rating: _____

3. If your children were asked to talk about the kind of parent you are today, what kinds of things might they say?

   Example: Mommy yells loud when I'm bad but she loves me no matter what. She puts me in time-out if I spill my juice because I'm being silly.

   Be as honest as you can, and write a brief description of yourself from your child's perspective.

   _____

   _____

   _____

   _____

   _____

   _____

4. Would you change your rating on the scale after using your child's viewpoint? If so, write down the new number and any thoughts you have about that. Revised rating: _____

   _____

   _____

   _____

   _____

5. What would you need to change to make things match up better?

    For example: *I need to yell less and be more patient. I need to find more time to play.*

    _____

    _____

    _____

    _____

6. If your children are old enough, you could ask them to describe you after you have finished the exercise. Be prepared for them to remember things differently than you do and try not to lead their answers (for example, "You like how Mommy tucks you in, right?"). Use their comments to guide you, not hurt you. Do not let this turn into a relationship-damaging exercise!

    My child's version:

    _____

    _____

    _____

    _____

    _____

    _____

    _____

Awareness helps us recognize if we have gone off course and helps us adjust to get back on course. Use this information to help you recognize any areas of misalignment between the parent you wanted to be and the parent you are today.

Chapter 2: Believe It or Not

My Inheritance

When I was young, my family always got excited about having a real Christmas tree. A couple times we all trekked out into the middle of nowhere in search of the perfect tree. On these occasions, our toes would freeze and frustrations would rise as my three siblings and I would tire of the deep snow and fuss about going back home. The tree we chose always seemed to have a nest in it, stink like an animal's toilet, or not fit on the roof of our car. Even when we bought a tree off a lot, there were problems.

Despite these memories, when my husband and I got married, I insisted we bring a real tree into our house. This seemed strange to my husband because I tend to resist killing things and especially love trees. Because my husband had no strong feelings one way or the other, he complied and out we'd go to pick up our tree.

Every year, the tree would fall over. Gifts were crushed, water was spilled, ornaments were broken, and needles would become embedded in the carpet to jab into my feet months after the tree was gone. Every stand we purchased developed a crack, and for many years our carpet would be marked from where the tree had stood. The aroma of the tree was often overwhelming for me, and I counted the days until it could be removed from my house.

One day, I read an article by Dave Barry that outlined the reasons he disliked real Christmas trees. I found myself laughing and agreeing with every word. Suddenly, I realized that I was insisting on a real tree for no other reason than I had grown up with one. I had inherited a belief that was guiding my behaviour even though it conflicted with my likes and dislikes.

That year, we switched to an artificial tree, and I've never looked back. I still enjoy seeing real trees in other people's homes but am content to go home to my odorless artificial. More important, this whole experience made me think about what else I might have inherited and how those beliefs might still be influencing how I behave.

What Are We Really Up Against?

Kids today are different than we were: less respectful, more street-savvy, under greater pressure to succeed with easier access to drugs and other negative things.

A statement similar to this often comes up in groups of parents and is usually pronounced with much concern and more than a tinge of fear. Parents around the room nod their heads, agreeing that today's kids are out of control and too violent. They blame television and video games among other things, and share stories from every corner of the world. They are not talking about their own children but rather of the generation as a whole. I have a couple of thoughts on this way of thinking.

First, when we are talking about a generation of kids, we are talking about our own child, whether we think we are or not. We cannot talk about *kids these days* and then pretend our children are not part of that picture. They are. So, if we're going to talk about these kids as if they are defective and a menace to society let's be sure we understand our own precious little ones are in that group.

Second, have you ever noticed that whatever we focus on seems to expand in importance? For example, if you are thinking of buying a cute little red car that you think is unique and special, you will suddenly see hundreds of similar ones on the road. Or when you find out you're expecting a baby, you suddenly see pregnant women everywhere. These are examples of our filter system altering to allow this information in. It's not that pregnancies or red cars suddenly increased because of your interest. It's your awareness that has changed.

Let's take this one step further. What if it is more than just our awareness that increases? There are many great writers and speakers[1] who tell us that what we focus on truly does expand. If you've ever had an ache or pain and really given it all your attention, you've likely felt this expansion first hand. In parent education, we ask parents to focus on their child's positive behaviours or qualities. Parents are often amazed at how their child improves once they (the parents) are focused on the positives.

---

1   Louise Hay, Wayne Dyer, Abraham-Hicks, and Eckhart Tolle are just a few of the many who write or speak on this topic.

Whether we believe our focus makes things expand or only that our awareness makes things stand out, this is still an important concept to keep in mind.

So, what are we *really* up against? Are our children out of control and *different* than previous generations? Our kids are incredible. They are born knowing how to program televisions, DVD players, computers, and, most important, remote controls. The things they need to be aware of are different from those of generations past, but the basics have not changed. How else could our world continue to expand and thrive?

True, the younger generations have a different work ethic from what we are used to. They seem to put self-care above all else, and if they have a tickle in their throat they stay home. The older generations, like Baby Boomers and Generation X, went to work through rain, snow, sleet, and illness.

Maybe this change is a way to preserve human life on our planet, or perhaps it's the universe's way of balancing out the numbers. If we ignore our bodies, they eventually break down. It's hard to enjoy retirement, or anything else, when we are fighting disease. The younger generations have come equipped to recognize these messages and deal with them more positively.

> *FREE Parenting Tip: Our children are smart, strong, and fully capable of doing what they have come here to do. All we need to do is believe in them.*

It is natural to believe our generation knows best and anyone who does things differently is wrong. While the stories we hear might make it tempting to believe a huge problem is on the rise with future generations, there is nothing to indicate that this is true. Our kids are different, but in an evolved and necessary way. They are smart, capable, and able to do what they have come here to do.

As parents we need to work hard to model mutual respect, to teach our kids *how* to think, and to provide skills to help them make good, healthy choices in the future. That really isn't any different from generations past.

So let's focus on all the good things we hear about children today. Really look for it and talk about it. It's everywhere. What we are really up against is the pressure to think there is something wrong with our children. We can't afford to write off our children, and I don't believe we want to. Our kids will survive and thrive and make us proud if we hold tight to our power and believe in them.

Thinking Outside of the Box

Of all the things that cause us anxiety in our lifetime, the stress of fitting in socially and emotionally has to be one of the greatest. If we never worried how others perceive our thoughts or actions, life would be a lot easier. Unfortunately, most of us are unable to do this.

For example, some of us feel stressed if a friend drops in and our house is a mess. Others will stress about how they look, what they wear, whether or not their language is politically correct, or how their child's behaviour is going to reflect on them. It's the idea that others are judging us and finding us lacking that causes discomfort.

When Eleanor Roosevelt said, "No one can make us feel inferior without our consent" she was hitting on a pretty big idea. We are bothered by others judging us when we believe what they say to be at least partially true. If someone suggests we are a bad parent for letting our ten-year-old go to the park alone, it will only bother us if we believe it might be wrong. Their judgment makes no difference in our lives, except that it preys on our insecurities and results in bad feelings. In other words, we give their judgment meaning.

It is interesting that we are seeing an increase in disorders that result in children having an impaired ability to pick up on social cues from other people. In other words, these children do not care what others think. They are wired to be unaffected by the judgments of others and are quite content to do their own thing regardless of how others view them.

I'm not in any way trying to belittle the hardships these kids and their loved ones face, and I'm not suggesting this is all these disorders are about. But I am asking the question: What if their inability to care what others think is not the problem? What if that part of their makeup actually sets them up to accomplish more than our "socially conscious" thinking could ever allow us to do?

I realize this kind of thinking is different from what we've been taught...but maybe this "out of the box" thinking is worth exploring further.

As a Matter of Belief ... I Do!

The subconscious mind is interesting to learn about and can shed a lot of light on understanding why we do the things we do. For our purposes, it is helpful to understand that our behaviours and feelings are largely a result of our current thoughts, which are strongly influenced by our beliefs.[2] Here is a simpler way to represent this idea:

BELIEFS → THOUGHTS → FEELINGS→ BEHAVIOUR

In its simplest form, when our senses pick up on things happening around us, they send this information to our brain. This data travels through a filter system that starts with our beliefs. For example, if a bee lands on our arm and we believe that *bees always sting,* our thought might be "Get it off!" Panic surges through us, causing violent arm swinging and possible screaming. Using the same format that we used above, we can visualize this sequence in the following way:

Bees sting → "Get it off!" → Panic → Arm swinging/running/screaming

But what if instead our belief was that *bees sting only if threatened?* This belief might look like the following:

Bees sting if threatened → "I'm no threat" → Calm/curious → Shoo it away

There are many other ways this could look, but the point is that our belief greatly influences what we think and feel and how we react as a result.

Things don't always work in this linear fashion with beliefs determining the outcome. Sometimes we can change our thoughts about something and influence how we feel and behave. The consequence of

---

2   **Daniel Goleman, Stephen Covey, and Anthony Robbins are a few of my favorite authors on this topic.**

this changed thought will either strengthen or weaken our original belief.

Imagine that you are the panicked person just described. Let's say you go to an anxiety clinic to get over your fear. When the bee lands on you again, you would use the new thoughts you learned at the clinic to remain still. Now things might look something like this:

Bees always sting → "Stay calm, you're okay, breathe." → Anxious → Freeze

If the bee flies away without hurting you, it weakens your original belief and decreases the anxiety you'll feel the next time a bee lands on you. With practice and time you might completely shift your belief to *bees only sting if threatened.* (On the other hand, if the bee stings you despite your non-threatening behaviour, it will strengthen your old belief that *bees always sting,* and you might no longer trust the people at the anxiety clinic!)

The point is our beliefs have an influence on almost everything we do. Unless we consciously decide to think a different thought or feel a different way, our beliefs will ensure we get a lot of repeat behaviours in life.

Many beliefs are inherited from our family of origin (like my tree story) and sneak into our filter system without much thought at all. Others are formed as we repeat thoughts over and over in our mind or when we witness something traumatic.

Beliefs that are formed as a result of emotional trauma can be extremely strong, almost like they are burned into the mind. These beliefs can interfere with our daily lives because once recalled they trigger the strong thoughts, feelings, and behaviours that were present when the belief was created. Sorting through our beliefs becomes an important task that should be done slowly, in baby steps.

FREE Parenting Tip: Everything we see, hear, touch, taste, think, feel, and do is influenced by our belief system. These filters allow us to function but can also interfere with new information ... it makes sense to be aware of our beliefs.

Exercise: What Do You Believe?

Your beliefs around parenting (or any relationship) have a lot of influence on how you function, so it's a good idea to become aware of what they are. Included is a list of statements to help you identify beliefs in your life.

Your task is the following:

1. Decide whether or not you agree with the statements provided in the list at the end of this chapter ("Sample Beliefs"). Create a list of those you agree with or revise them to fit your own beliefs.

   _____

   _____

   _____

   _____

   _____

   _____

   _____

   _____

2. Rate how important each belief is to you using a scale of one to ten with ten being extremely important and one being not important at all.

3. Starting with the most important beliefs (tens) think about the following;

    a) Where does the belief come from?

    _____

    _____

    _____

    _____

    b) Why is it important to me?

    _____

    _____

    _____

    _____

    c) How am I enforcing it?

    _____

    _____

    _____

    _____

    d) What is it teaching?

    _____

    _____

    _____

    _____

4. If you have a partner helping you raise your children, do the lists separately and then compare and discuss them. If partners disagree on a belief, one way to deal with it is to look at the rating. If one partner rates something as a ten (very important) and the other rates it as a five (moderately important), you would defer to the one for whom it's very important. You might want to limit the number of "very important" beliefs allowed.

5. If your children are verbal, use this exercise to start a family discussion about beliefs. Be sure the reasons for each belief fits with family values and be open to making changes where "good reasons" are out of reach. You are passing on beliefs to your children all the time. It's nice to know what they are inheriting and why.

Sample Beliefs

- Kids need a set bedtime and must be in bed, lights out and quiet by that time.

- Kids should eat everything on their plate at dinner time.

- Dessert is available for everyone (regardless of the amount of supper they've eaten) but should be eaten after the meal.

- Kids should be given an allowance only if they have earned it.

- Television, computer, and electronic games should be limited in daily use.

- Kids should bath/shower daily, twice a week, weekly, monthly.

- Kids should have assigned chores by the age of _____ and should have consequences for not doing them.

- Kids should respect their elders and should not interrupt them.

- Violent games and shows should be restricted to kids ___years old and older.

- When kids misbehave, they are testing our boundaries.

- Mistakes should be learned from and therefore never repeated.

- A baby that is picked up when it cries becomes spoiled.

- Misbehaviours must be dealt with quickly and sternly.

- Children cannot make their own decisions about tattoos and body piercings until they're grown up.

- Kids' bedrooms are part of the house and should reflect that in their cleanliness.

- Kids should do what they are asked or told to do the first time they are asked or told.

- Grounding a child teaches responsibility and respect.

- If kids go outside improperly dressed, they can catch a cold.

- Tattoos and body piercings shouldn't be allowed before a certain age.

Chapter 3: This Is Your Body Speaking

My Lesson in Fear

When my kids were two and four, we were outside enjoying the sun. I was working in a garden and my kids were playing in the yard right behind me. Noticing things were quiet, I looked for my kids. I knew they could not have gone far in the moments since I'd last seen them. Scanning our small acreage with the pond in the back and fields on two sides, fear shot through me.

Calling their names, I walked the few feet to an old shed beside where I had last seen them. The dog raised her head to look at me, but everything else was quiet. I jogged around the shed, continuing to call their names, and then turned and ran into the house. I ran upstairs, back to the main floor, downstairs, but all I heard was my own panting. By now, my heart was in my throat and my memory was pulling out every story I'd ever heard about kids getting lost in cornfields, drowning in ponds, getting run over by gravel trucks or carried off by coyotes.

I knew these scenarios were unlikely, but my rational thinking was gone.

Running back outside, my eyes zeroed in on our dog lying beside the old shed. That was odd as she was always with the kids. With tears in my eyes and a catch in my throat, I told the dog to find the kids. In response I heard one tiny giggle.

My fear evaporated into relief then transformed into outrage. The kids came out from behind a board in the shed, giggling. I looked down at their smiling faces, a million thoughts of what to do crashing in my mind. The dog placed herself in between me and the kids as if sensing my surging emotions and loss of control.

Overwhelmed by my thoughts and emotions I sat down and started to cry. The giggling stopped and a little hand tried to push up my head. "Mommy, you otay? We fooled you, wight?"

"Yes," I muttered in between sobs. "You fooled me."

When I was able to talk, I told them how important they are to me and how scared I was that something bad had happened to them. We hugged and they patted my back soothingly. From that day on we only played hide-and-seek after announcing the game first.

The "F" Word

It's time to discuss the "F" word: Feelings. This is about our internal guidance system that protects us and prepares us for battle. It involves body cues or physiological changes in the body that are constantly checking in to find out how "safe" we are at any given moment.

Many people talk about feelings as if they are a "fluffy" topic that we should pay attention to only when forced to by a therapist or hormonal woman. When we use this sort of approach, we are ignoring our natural guidance system and setting ourselves up for surprise reactions. Feelings are closely tied to two other "f" words, *flight* and *fight*, as they act like a security system for these responses by alerting us that something is wrong.

In the past, our feelings were a major part of our survival system. If we came across a saber tooth tiger, fear would shoot through us accompanied by a thought like "Get out of here quick!" The brain, which has no access to the outside world, would acknowledge this information and ask our external sensors (eyes, ears, nose, or skin) to confirm the danger signal. If our senses confirmed it, blood and oxygen would immediately be diverted from our vital organs, including the thinking part of our brain, to activate the "fight-or-flight" response team (the primitive brain and our limbs).[3] This would provide greater strength and speed to help us run away, climb a tree, or prepare to fight.

Stated simply, when our body thinks we are in danger, blood is sent to the areas responsible for strength and speed. The brain (and other vital organs) are deprived of blood until the danger subsides. This is necessary for survival, because even a really smart person isn't going to be much good once he's in the belly of a tiger.

We are not at our smartest when this survival system kicks in, yet most of the situations we face today require more thought and less strength and speed. The decisions we make in the heat of the moment

---

3   **Lipton, Bruce. H.,** *The Wisdom of Your Cells: How Your Beliefs Control Your Biology* **(Sounds True Audio Learning, 2007).**

might seem fitting at the time, but once our thinking brain is back in charge, they rarely look as good.

Our main job becomes recognizing our feelings, not just fear and anger, but all kinds of feelings—embarrassment, humiliation, disappointment, irritation, worry, passion, excitement, enthusiasm, etc. When we recognize these feelings (there are plenty of body cues), it is our job to provide useful and relevant feedback to our brain so we can respond accordingly.

The good news is that while it is our senses that provide the information, most feedback is given by our thoughts and we control our thoughts. The bad news is that we have learned so many negative responses and thinking patterns that we often get caught up in negative thought patterns and send back the wrong message.

For example, let's pretend someone you want to impress is on her way over to your place for dinner. Ten minutes before she arrives, your child spills grape juice all over the beige carpet in the entranceway. It is the first thing your guest will see when she arrives. As you watch the purple stain grow on the carpet, shock, anger, and disappointment surge through you.

"Am I in danger?" your brain asks. You look at your son, the stain, the clock, and unbidden thoughts come to mind. "I don't believe it! This is terrible. I told him this was an important evening for me. He's not even supposed to have juice in this room. Everything is ruined!" The message the brain receives is, "Yes, I am in danger. Get ready to fight." Blood is diverted and you are no longer thinking at your best.

On the other hand, if you learn to recognize your body tension, rapid breathing, and clenched fists, you can short-circuit the negative loop with a thought like, "Everything is okay, there is no danger." Then you can take a deep breath, relax your tense muscles, and really think about what you need to do. The carpet might be ruined, but no amount of foot-stomping, yelling, or threatening is going to change that.

Sometimes it is the body cues themselves that make us uncomfortable and cause us to "fly off the handle." We feel the tension in our back, the butterflies in our stomach and the slightly increased heart rate. What we don't notice is that these body cues are like questions checking to see if we need to get ready to protect ourselves. If we ignore this piece of the equation, lower-level feelings, such as disappointment, nervousness and frustration, can result in a response that seems way out of proportion.

Tuning in to our body cues and recognizing what those feelings are all about allows us to use our guidance system properly. Let's reclaim this "f" word and teach our children to be aware of this incredible message system. We can support it openly by learning about our physiological changes and celebrating the fact that we are aware. Feelings, feelings, Rah! Rah! Rah!

FREE Parenting Tip: Children are not saber tooth tigers; when we understand the body cues that come with our feelings, we can avoid a primitive response to their actions.

Tuning In to Our Signals

If we want to teach our children how to embrace their feelings and become more self-aware, we must start by tuning into our own. One of the simplest ways to teach self-awareness is to talk about our feelings and help our kids to talk about theirs. There are hundreds of words to describe different feelings we experience, each involving subtle differences in our body cues and eventual response. If you haven't used a lot of feeling words in the past, you might start by using a variety of new feeling words to describe what's going on for you.

FREE Parenting Tip: Being self-aware means knowing how different emotions feel in our body and taking the time to figure out what's causing them. When we do this, we make it easier to model self-control and respond in a suitable way.

Tuning in also means learning which feelings (for example, embarrassment, disappointment, fear, worry, jealousy) make us more reactive. Feelings are only signals, yet sometimes they trigger a much stronger response. For example, many of us dislike being embarrassed and will quickly get angry when something embarrasses us. Many students will admit they blew up at their teacher after feeling embarrassed. The teacher might not have been involved in the embarrassing moment, but it was that feeling that made the student lose his self-control.

Understanding how and why we react to different feelings makes it easier to maintain self-control. For example, if we recognize the body cues for being embarrassed and learn to see the humor in a situation (and even point it out to others), we can vent the emotion through laughter rather than yelling. It's worth it to figure out our sensitive areas and develop healthy ways to deal with them.

How Are You Feeling?

Accepting	Critical	Furious	Lucky	Revengeful
Aggravated	Curious	Giddy	Mad	Righteous
Agitated	Depressed	Grievous	Mean	Sad
Alive	Disappointed	Grounded	Mellow	Sassy
Angry	Disconnected	Grumpy	Mischievous	Scared
Anxious	Embarrassed	Guilty	Moody	Self conscious
Ashamed	Empowered	Happy	Nervous	Sensitive
Awestruck	Empty	Honoured	Nice	Special
Awkward	Encouraged	Humiliated	Obstinate	Smart
Balanced	Energized	Hurt	Ordinary	Smitten
Blessed	Enlightened	Hurtful	Overwhelmed	Strengthened
Bored	Enraged	Impatient	Panicked	Strong
Brave	Entertained	Included	Paranoid	Successful
Brilliant	Envious	Invigorated	Patient	Tense
Calm	Evil	Invisible	Peaceful	Terrific
Careless	Excited	Involved	Petty	Terrified
Challenged	Excluded	Inspired	Picky	Threatened
Concerned	Fabulous	Irrational	Picked on	Thrilled
Confused	Fearful	Irritated	Placated	Tolerant
Connected	Flustered	Jealous	Playful	Unbalanced
Contemplative	Forgotten	Jumpy	Popular	Uninhibited
Content	Free	Left out	Proud	Unique
Controlled	Friendly	Lonely	Quiet	Upbeat
Cooperative	Frightened	Lost	Rational	Vulnerable
Crazy	Frustrated	Loved	Relaxed	Wacky
Creative	Fun	Love struck	Resentful	Worried

The feelings that arise from unmet expectations are a common cause of loss of control and a big part of tuning in to self-awareness. For example, imagine you come home to a sleeping household after a long, tough day. The kitchen, which was spotless when you left, is now a mess. You clean it up grumbling about how unappreciative your family is and how you have to do everything.

The next morning, your teenage son saunters into the kitchen asking for lunch money and informing you he needs a ride to his friend's house after school today. You lose it. "What do you think I am, a bank? And who said you could go out after school, you hardly do anything around here and then just expect me to drop everything so I can drive you everywhere?"

Seeing the look on his face, you realize you've misstepped and quickly shift into damage control, but he's no longer talking or listening.

What caused this eruption? This blaming stance came from the fact you were still holding on to unresolved feelings from the night before. In other words, the feelings that arose when you walked into the kitchen last night were still lurking and sent you flying off the handle with the slightest provocation.

If you had considered what caused those feelings back when they originally arose, you might have realized your family had not met your expectations. This might have led you to plan a family meeting to discuss expectations and sharing of the workload. People cannot meet your expectations if they don't know what they are. Alternatively, your thinking might have helped you see that you were frustrated with your job, for keeping you out late, more than with your family.

Identifying the cause of a feeling helps us keep things in perspective and deal with things calmly and assertively. Sometimes we'll expose unrealistic expectations or a communication breakdown, while at other times we'll unveil much bigger problems (for example, work hours or marital problems). In any case, these situations will be teaching our kids how to tune in to their signals, helping them to be less reactive and more self-aware.

Statements to Teach Self-Awareness:

"I'm really disappointed that Grandma cancelled. I was so excited that she was coming."

"That music is irritating me, and I'm finding it hard to concentrate."

"I feel jittery. I guess I'm anxious for the games to begin."

"This bickering is exasperating to listen to. I can feel the tension in my shoulders."

"I can tell by your jaw you're getting angry."

"I'm getting frustrated. Maybe we should both stop and relax a bit before we continue."

"When I get nervous, I'm uncomfortable and get angry easier. Maybe we should wait until after my job interview to discuss this."

"I'm tense because of my exams tomorrow. I'm sorry I snapped at you—it wasn't your fault."

"It's okay to be angry—it's not okay to hit."

"I feel guilty that I never took you to the zoo as promised. I can see you're disappointed. How can I make that up to you?"

"I'm frustrated that this toy is so hard to put together. I better take a break before I throw it across the room."

"I'm getting a headache from being so nervous. I need to take a few deep breaths and relax."

"I'm sorry you didn't win the award. I understand how disappointing that can be."

"I feel sad we can't keep the puppy at our place. Maybe one day they'll find a cure for allergies."

Exercise: Taking Charge of Your Body

An important part of becoming self-aware is recognizing what's going on in our bodies and talking about that with our kids. Our body cues are unique for each of us, but there is often enough commonality to make a connection. For example, some people will feel tension in their jaw when they are angry, while others will notice it more in their shoulders. Tension is a common cue for anger; however, where it surfaces for each of us can be different. Work through the following exercise alone or with your children.

Think of three situations in which you overreacted emotionally and later regretted.

Write down what you were feeling in each situation.

For example: *Yelled at my son for ripping his new pants—angry, disappointed, frustrated*

———————————————————————————

———————————————————————————

———————————————————————————

Create a list of the body cues that occurred. Think about tension, your hands, your face, if you were hot or cold, if you had any twitches, etc. Write down everything you can think of for each feeling.

For example: *Angry—hot face, clenched jaw, tight shoulders, clenched fists, volcano in belly.*

Feeling: ——————————————————————

———————————————————————————

———————————————————————————

Feeling: ——————————————————————

———————————————————————————

———————————————————————————

Feeling: ——————————————————————

———————————————————————————

———————————————————————————

Look at each situation separately and try to remember what you were thinking before the reaction, and write it down:

For example: *I don't have any money left until payday, and now he's ruined the one thing I purchased that was going to last. He's so ungrateful ... just doesn't appreciate all I do.*

_____

_____

_____

_____

_____

_____

_____

Create at least three thoughts you could use in future situations to tell your brain you are not in danger and to help you stay calm.

For example: *Take a deep breath, I doubt he did it on purpose, it's okay.*

_____

_____

_____

_____

_____

For the rest of the week, try to notice your emotions as they arise and, when possible, take a moment to reflect on the cues associated with it. Sometimes just recognizing the signals are there is enough to keep you thinking positive.

Chapter 4: Getting Back on Course

My Moment of Clarity

When my son was three, we purchased a papasan chair for my office. One day, I noticed something white on the wood of the chair. Upon closer inspection, I saw that someone had marked the soft wood along one side. I put the clues together: My kids and I had been sitting in the chair reading an hour earlier. Since then, my son had brought me a key he'd found, which was sitting on my desk. My daughter was napping. It was obvious that my son was the culprit.

With anger and disbelief surging through my body, I called my son over. "What happened here?" I asked, clenching my jaw tightly.

"I don't know," he responded, looking at the floor. Knowing he was lying would normally have increased my anger, but instead it had the opposite effect. I realized that he was afraid of my anger and didn't feel it was safe to tell me the truth. That bothered me and stopped my anger in its tracks. I took a deep breath and sat down beside the chair. Opening my hand, I showed him the key.

"Do you know what I think happened?" I asked in a gentle voice.

"What?" he asked, risking a quick look at my face.

"I think someone found a key and accidentally scratched it against this chair. Then, when he found it scratched really easy and was kind of fun, he decided to make more scratches. By the time he realized that what he was doing might be a problem, the chair was all marked up." I paused, watching him ponder my assessment.

"I'm sorry, Mommy," he said, his eyes full of tears. "I didn't mean to do it."

I took him in my arms and we sat together, talking about what we could do to fix this. We decided to use brown marker and cover up the scratches together. It worked pretty well, and I think we both learned something valuable that day.

What's the Big Idea?

When things happen in life that we don't like, we automatically think about how we would like it to be instead. These upsets provide contrast and allow us to envision a better world. This simple process is enough to make us feel better, if we allow those feelings in. Unfortunately, most of us experience something we don't like, envision what we'd like to have happen instead, and then hold on to the frustrated feelings that came with the initial situation. In other words, we don't feel better because of our vision—if anything we make ourselves feel worse.

This is a challenging concept to understand, especially when it comes to dealing with our children. What it is saying is that when our children misbehave, we have two choices. We can focus on their current behaviour and allow it to upset us, or we can envision them behaving the way we would prefer, feel the relief that comes with that vision, and hold tight to that feeling. In other words, it is to our benefit to pretend they are behaving in a good way, so we can hold on to that positive feeling! This is very hard for us to do.

When we see our child behave in a way we do not like and we focus on this action, negative emotions surface inside of us. When we feel these kinds of emotions, our brain starts checking to see if something is wrong. If we let our thoughts go unchecked, we will start giving back the signal that something is wrong and everything moves in a negative direction.

When we refuse to go with the negative, but instead keep our focus on the feelings that come with the positive ideal, we are not burying our heads in the sand, but shifting our focus from negative to positive. This helps us to keep things in perspective and also makes the positives of the situation stand out. Our child unconsciously feels this shift in energy and will begin to behave in a more positive way, which is what we wanted to have happen in the first place.

Unconditional love is about loving someone regardless of condition. In other words, when our child is behaving badly, we still love her. We may not like her current behaviour, but we still love her. If we focus on that love, it truly becomes unconditional.

Strategies That Help Us Focus on the Big Idea

Most of us want to be good parents. When other people are around us, we will tone down our parenting responses to match what we feel is socially acceptable. For example, it is rare to see a parent spank her child in public today. Does this mean parents no longer spank? No, while spanking seems to be on the decrease, there are still many parents who spank their child in the privacy of their own home.

Because of this toning down in public, I often suggest parents pretend they have someone they admire watching them when their children are misbehaving. By doing this, they remain aware of their responses and are able to keep the big picture in mind.

Some parents find this too hard to do when their child is pushing their buttons. For these parents, I suggest they try out their acting ability and imagine they are auditioning for a role in a movie. The child playing the role opposite them is supposed to get them angry in the movie, but their character must remain calm and controlled. Some people find this idea helpful as it allows them to stay focused on their performance rather than getting caught up in what their child is trying to do.

Another role we can play is that of a reporter. If we pretend it is our job to figure out, and report on, what is really bothering our child, we will put effort into helping him calm down. This involves turning judgment into curiosity and instead of allowing anger to guide our interaction, we put our energy into understanding our child better.

A final suggestion to help keep us focused on the big idea is to develop some tricks that will lower our heart rate whenever we feel things start to rocket. It might be singing a favorite song, reciting a rhyme, repeating an affirmation, or humming a tune—anything that will help us center on ourselves rather than escalate things with our child. When we stay calm, we have an anchoring influence on our child and are creating a big idea we can be proud of.

> *FREE Parenting Tip: When we focus on the positives, and the feelings that vision creates, we are putting our energy into making that happen. This helps us stay calmer, deal with the situation better, and demonstrate unconditional love for our child.*

Finding Our Way

Sometimes, after becoming aware of our parenting picture, we parents feel as if we are so lost we might as well give up. I guarantee you this is not the case. Raising a family is much like flying an airplane. The plane is slightly off course ninety percent of the time, but because the pilot knows where he is headed, the plane will still make it to its destination.

The first thing to keep in mind is that we are doing the best we can with what we know at that moment in time. There is no reason to waste energy blaming ourselves, our kids, or anyone else for challenges in our family environment. You have everything you need to do this job. Don't allow anyone to make you believe differently. Resources like reading material, counselors, or parent educators can help you prepare for the trip, but you are in charge of the journey. So start wherever your family is currently at, and believe in your ability to get the job done.

The second thing to remember is that children are extremely resilient and forgiving. Even teenagers who talk like they hate their parents are usually hoping for a ceasefire. If your kids are older, it will take more effort to get everyone working together, but it is still possible.

While every family is different, there are some basic ideas that can help relationships get back on track:

- Start by envisioning your family the way you want it to be. Don't limit yourself to what you think is possible, but really allow your dream to take shape.

- Decide what *you* can do to make your vision come to life. The only thing we truly have control over is ourselves, so that is where we must start.

- With your energy focused on yourself, start making little changes. Although you might be the only one putting in an effort at this point, you will still see positive results.

Building Relationships

Our relationships with other people involve a lot of give and take. When we are kind, supportive, complimentary, etc., we give to the relationship. When we are critical, demanding, nagging, etc., we take away from it. Over time, our relationships become stronger or weaker depending on this give-and-take ratio.[4]

When a relationship is strong, it is okay to tease about a mistake. However, that same teasing can result in hurt feelings or negative reactions when a relationship is weak. This does not mean we can never

---

4   **Stephen Covey's Emotional Bank Account in** *The 7 Habits of Highly Effective Families* **provides a great analogy for relationship give-and-take.**

make fun of people, but to make it enjoyable we must be aware of how generally strong or weak our relationship with them is at that time.

Take a look at the chart outlining relationship building and give some thought to how much time you spend giving and taking.

These ideas are not exhaustive, but they are a great place to start.[5] As with most things in life, the game of give-and-take is all about balance. If you are in a relationship with anyone—kids, spouse, neighbour, colleague—that is feeling strained, try focusing on building that relationship for a week. If you focus on strengthening the relationship and avoiding anything that weakens it, you will notice a change for the better.

> *FREE Parenting Tip: We can get our family back on course by figuring out where we want to be headed, taking baby steps to make positive changes in that direction, and putting energy into strengthening our relationships.*

---

5   **Sam Horn's book** *Tongue Fu!* **provides excellent examples of words that shut down communication versus those that enhance and support it.**

Building Relationships: The Game of Give-and-Take

Things that build a strong relationship	Things that weaken a relationship
• Compliments	• Insults, teasing, putdowns
• Effective feedback and using supportive statements	• Eye-rolling, sneers
• Pat on the back, wink, high-five	• Recoiling or pulling (rudely) away from a touch
• Smiles	• "Shoulding on" a person— you should have …You should know better …
• Listening and sharing	
• Remembering important details	
• Giving a genuine apology	• Providing unsolicited advice
• Making and keeping promises	• Physical hurt; hitting, pinching, ear-tweaking, pushing
• Acts of kindness—doing something special for that person "just because"	
	• Threatening, intimidation
• Using a voice that projects kindness and understanding	• Yelling or swearing at the person
• I believe in you messages "I know you can handle this, you can do anything," etc	• Breaking promises without compensation
	• "You'll never do it; you're not good/big/strong enough"
• Laughing together	• Laughing at the person
• Standing up for that person even when he is not present	• Gossip/disloyalty—making fun of someone or telling stories about him

Counting on Success

People need at least four successes for every failure in order to want to try. If this doesn't happen, a person often decides to stop trying altogether. If we want him to start trying again, we need to find a way to build in successes for him. We can lower the bar on what we see as successful, but true success is not about compliments or encouraging statements.

When a person stops trying, he will often do something to ensure failure, adopting the attitude that "I will fail you before you fail me," or what I call the "f-you attitude."

When a person reaches this point, he is hurting. The only way to get out of a hole is to climb, but he is refusing to do so. We can allow him to sit in his hole until he decides he doesn't like it there and begins to climb out. When he does start to climb, he will find us waiting on the rim (where we've been all along) ready to support and encourage him. If we can do this while maintaining an optimistic attitude, we can have a very positive influence on this process.

One thing we need to avoid when our kids are feeling this way is our tendency to pass him a shovel and make him dig deeper. This happens if we are being critical and reminding him he is not measuring up in our judgment. (For example: "Why can't you just try? I don't understand why you keep giving up. I've never given up on anything in my life."). This just confirms what he has already decided is true: he is a failure.

Finally, no matter how badly we might want to do it, we cannot lift our child out of the hole. If we do, he will likely dig another deeper one.

So whether we have lost our way or are currently dealing with a child in a hole, there are always things we can do to make a difference. Parenting is a work in progress. By becoming aware of what we can do to help our family find its way, we are doing the best we can with what we know—and who can ask for better than that?

Exercise: Setting Life Priorities

You are ninety years old, sitting in a rocking chair looking back over your life. Think about the things in your childhood that made you feel safe, secure, and happy. Watch your life play out before you like a film highlighting successes and failures. Zero in on the moment you find out you are going to be a parent. Think about the feelings this news creates for you. What are your dreams or wishes for the future?

Continue to move forward in time. Your kids are growing. How do you treat them? What kinds of things do you do to help them feel safe, secure, and loved? Look at the balance in your life: How much do you work ... play ... stop to just enjoy? Your kids idolize you. Can you hear them talking about you to their friends? What are they saying?

Keep on traveling forward. Your kids are moving out, maybe marrying or having children of their own. How do they treat you, their partner, their kids? Do they like you? Is work dominating their lives? Do they come to visit you? If so, do they do it because they want to? Do they still talk about you? What are they saying now?

You've reached retirement and moved into old age. How important is your job to you now? Do your previously close colleagues still call? Do you feel like a valued member of society? You are ninety looking back. Do you like what you see?

If you could write your whole story, what would you change? While there might be things that seem impossible to adjust in your life, there are little things you can do to guide your life in the direction you would prefer to go.

Sticking to priorities is a tough task for all of us. Life seems so urgent most of the time, but if we don't live now, when will we?

Part 2

Understanding You and Your Family

Chapter 5: Where Did *That* Come From?

My Tween Adjustment

My daughter has always been very determined and clear on what she does or doesn't want to do. These qualities have forced me to adapt the way I do things and taught me a whole new level of communication. I am convinced she was put on this earth to keep me honest and to remind me to use my skills every step of the way.

When my daughter entered the preteen stage, things started to change and I found myself dealing with a girl who was often angry, sarcastic, and condescending. Our close, loving relationship appeared to be in danger, and while I wasn't shocked by this change, I wasn't happy about it either.

After a while, I noticed it affecting my behaviour in a negative way. I found I didn't want to be around her and sometimes would avoid sharing information with her to steer clear of drama. On other occasions I would make a half-hearted attempt to negotiate, compromise, or explain something to her, and if she didn't cooperate immediately, I'd pull out my Parent Power to get my way. I felt like I was constantly nagging, correcting, threatening to remove privileges, or snapping at her. It was a frustrating time, and I didn't like it.

Eventually, I realized that although puberty for her and mid-life for me were at least partly to blame, there had to be a better way to do this. At this rate, we wouldn't be talking by the end of the year, and she was only eleven.

One day I cornered her and told her we had to talk about our relationship. She rolled her eyes, but to her credit she agreed. We shut ourselves in a room for a "Girls' Club"[6] meeting and launched into discussion. I told her that I had never been the mom of a young woman before and that I didn't have a clue what was the right or wrong way to go about things. I let her know I understood she was going through lots of changes and told her I was dealing with changes of my own. I went on to say our relationship was far too precious for me to let it be destroyed and that I liked her and missed having our special moments together.

We talked for about an hour, and to my surprise she agreed with me. She told me she didn't like being bossed around all the time and that I always seemed so critical of her. "Sometimes I don't even want to come and sit in the same room as you," she said, "because I know within five seconds you'll be assigning me a chore or pointing out something I did wrong."

---

6   Girls' club is something either of us can call at any time to announce we need private time to talk together. No subject is off limits, and nothing said there can be shared with others (except in this special case).

That conversation turned our relationship around, and I believe saved us from going to a dark and ugly place. We still have little moments of disagreement, and I have to work hard to keep up my end of the bargain. I'm not perfect at it yet and doubt I ever will be. I have, however, successfully graduated from mother to mentor. I am more self-aware, and once again am enjoying spending time with my daughter.

What We Don't Know Can Hurt Us

There are many factors that combine to make us the wonderful, unique people we are. Understanding or at least being aware of these factors is important because it helps us relate to others and create realistic expectations.

There are two major forces to be aware of when it comes to establishing who we have become: what nature has provided and what has been nurtured into us. The first idea focuses on those things we are born with—personality type, learning styles, communication modes, and things along those lines. These things will always be with us, although we can learn ways to work with them so we control them more than they control us.

The second influence focuses on how our environment affects who we are and the kinds of things we do in our lives. The family environment we were raised in is a big factor in this area, as our upbringing has instilled in us many beliefs, thought patterns, and behaviours. In fact, many of the things we think, say, and do with our own kids will be based on what our caregivers did with us—unless we make a conscious effort to do otherwise. Although the environmental impact also includes things like traumatic events, eye-opening moments, and influence from our teachers, mentors, role models, and friends, it is our family of origin that tends to have the biggest overall effect on us.

Natures versus nurture discussions have been going on for a long time with both sides giving valid reasons for which kind of influence is most important. The reality is that both nature and nurture shape who we are. Which side influences us more isn't as important as becoming aware of how these things affect us, so we can be the person, and have the family, we've always envisioned.

It Runs in the Family

When we talk about family types, it is important to remember that the possible structures and factors influencing how they will look are pretty much endless. The stressors our families endure, the support system we have, and the generation we are raised in are just a few of the things that will make a difference. It is easier to discuss the extreme family types and then focus on the kind of blends we might create to make it work for us[7].

The things we do with our own kids will be influenced by the family we grew up in. Some of these things we might have consciously decided to avoid or include in our family life, while others will be unconsciously occurring. If we are not aware of how our family of origin influences us, it can be very frustrating and guilt-producing when we behave in certain ways.

The first extreme in families is the *my way or the highway* type which is governed by strict, inflexible rules. It follows the authoritarian

---

7   **Barbara Coloroso's book** *Kids Are Worth It!* **provides a thorough and fun discussion on family types.**

model of *because I said so* and offers little explanation as to why these rules are important. There are strict consequences for breaking rules, and punishment is often the norm. It tends to be one person who leads in this family and anyone who dares to challenge that person is seen as disrespectful and in need of a lesson. When a strong-willed child or a child challenged by social cues is born into a family like this, the rule-maker will strive to make this child comply even if breaking his or her will is the only way to do this.

This type of family does not like other people being involved in their business and gets very upset if family members share information with people outside of the home. Physical punishments like slapping, arm pulling, pinching, or pushing are common, as are threats, groundings, and privilege removal. In this house, you are taught *what* to think rather than how to think for yourself.

The other extreme is the *loosey-goosey* type of family that adopts a very permissive style of parenting. Chaos thrives in this environment, as boundaries are not clearly laid out and are rarely enforced. Rules are few and far between and can change with the stress of the moment. This parent will often plead for compliance and will use guilt-laden statements to get her way. She will make threats, feel bad for making the threats, and try to make up for it by buying gifts or not following through with the punishment.

Consistency does not exist in this family and the roles people play (leader, follower, rule-maker) can jump around from person to person. A strong-willed child in this home will often try to take over, but in their youth will have trouble dealing with difficult adult decisions. In this house, you are loved when you are good and made to feel guilty or bad when you are not.

In either of these extremes, major problems arise. Too much structure makes one crave flexibility, while too little structure results in a desire for order and predictability. When people are raised in these environments, they often vow to raise their children the opposite way. Unfortunately, this doesn't work, because the opposite environment is not desirable either. Tension will arise due to the lack of order or rigid structure, resulting in inconsistent follow-through and lack of mutual respect. This flipflop way of living causes anxiety, confusion, guilt, or anger and can make parents feel like failures or believe their kids are bad beyond repair.

Creating a Balanced Family

Thankfully, most of us were not raised in either of these extremes but instead have grown up in a blend of our own. What's important is that we become aware of the pieces of our family of origin that influence the way we parent today and do not fit with our vision of the kind of parent we would like to be.

In an ideal world, a balanced family has a few well thought out rules with the flexibility to make new ones as the need arises. Their home environment is built on fairness and consistency, with clear boundaries and consequences for breaking them. When problems arise they would be discussed and worked through in a way that teaches everyone how to think for themselves. All members of the household are expected to follow the rules, and if problems are continually surfacing, the rule itself might be revamped.

This family type is flexible and works to build mutual respect using a variety of discipline tools and communication skills. People are loved and accepted for who they are and provided with the guidance and support to meet their full potential.

In reality, few—if any—of us would fit perfectly into this balanced family mold, and if we did we wouldn't stay there for long. Life is about finding balance, not about being perfectly balanced all the time. Growing and learning, as well as independence and confidence, grow out of imbalance and the efforts we take to fix it.

The exercise at the end of this chapter can be used to help figure out where your family is today so you can become aware and continue building the kind of family you really want.

> *FREE Parenting Tip: Your family of origin influences your family of creation. Identify the things that were done in your upbringing that you would prefer not to repeat, and use that information to guide you in making changes with your current family.*

Let's Get Personal

The nature-related aspects of who we are—those qualities we were born with—stay relatively consistent throughout life. These qualities include our temperament or personality and predispose us to certain behaviours. They influence who or what we gravitate toward and can even determine health risks.

Temperament is genetic and has a large influence on our natural behaviour. When we learn to do something that goes against our natural tendency (for example, organize our desk despite a natural desire to live in clutter), we will find that when we are stressed we revert back to our true nature. This doesn't mean we can never change aspects of how we behave, but it does mean there are certain behaviours that will resurface throughout our lives.

Every personality type has positive traits and challenging traits. Learning which traits apply to the individuals in our families can help guide our expectations and discipline strategies. Knowing that our three-year-old thrives on organization can help explain why he has a temper tantrum after we carelessly push his toys to the end of the table at supper time. It can also help us recognize that he will not calm down and eat until we let him straighten things back out. Similarly, being aware of the social needs of our teenager can help us determine the best type of discipline to use with her and determine which skills to model to help her be successful with friends.

Where it stops being helpful is when we use this information to limit our child or use it as an excuse for allowing undesirable behaviours. Temperament is only one piece of the puzzle, and it serves us best when we remember that. Our children will always benefit from being taught social and emotional skills. Knowing their possible gaps helps us determine which areas to focus on first.

Many personality tests put people into four main categories while recognizing that a variety of blends are likely to surface. Although a small percentage of the population will share qualities from all four groupings, most people find that one or two categories describe them best. Outlined below are four main temperaments loosely based on a personality model called DISC.[8]

---

8   **William Moulton Marston is credited with writing the original DISC works under the title** *Emotions of Normal People* **in 1928.**

The Determined Driver: This person is a very strong, independent, leader type. He likes to be in charge and will often tell people what to do. He is results-oriented and wants to see things done even if it means the quality suffers. Full of energy, he tends to be in a hurry, holds pointed conversations, and is unconcerned about offending others. Empathy does not come naturally to him. A good argument strengthens him, and while he may be quick to get angry, he cools down just as fast. He is not likely to take things personally and rarely believes something is his fault (for example, "He shouldn't have made me mad."). He likes to know what is going to happen and is more focused on goals than on people.

A strong Determined Driver child will need his own space and stuff to really be happy. He will require clear boundaries and will need to be allowed to make choices. Use short, pointed messages with this child that focus on *what* needs to be done versus *whom* or *how* others are affected.

This child may need to be taught how to think of others' feelings and will likely only engage in those teachings if you briefly explain what it will do for his future. (For example, "To run a company someday, you'll need to be able to think of others' feelings."). These kids like to lead and take command of situations easily and quickly. They enjoy watching people disagree and often need help learning social skills like patience, empathy, and tolerance. Discipline works best when enforced consistently, calmly, and quickly with this child. Taking possessions from this child gets a strong reaction, while lectures do not. Remember, these kids love arguing and will look for any opportunity to get you riled up.

The Flamboyant Expressive: This person also has a very strong personality, but the focus is on people versus the task at hand. She loves fun and despises being controlled by others. She is a social butterfly who flits from group to group entertaining everyone in her flight path. She is imaginative, and while she likes to control others, is not very good at it due to her disorganized nature. She tends to struggle with time management and is notoriously late, even for her own events. She talks a lot and can overwhelm others with her force of character. People with this personality typically have good intentions, but are not great at follow-through which makes them appear scattered and inconsistent. They like to know *who* is involved rather than *what* is going to happen.

Kids who are Flamboyant Expressives have lots of friends, and social interaction will be the focus of their existence. They live in a world of disorganization, although will often be able to find what they need within that mess. They require reminders regarding time commitments and will be motivated by *who* will be involved (for example, "There will be lots of other kids at the daycare to play with.") versus what fun things they'll be doing (crafts, reading) once there. They enjoy planning social events, although they often need a helper to assist with organization. They can struggle with commitment as they might sign up for things because of the people involved and then decide they don't like that activity at all.

A Flamboyant Expressive child is closely connected to her friends and will rebel if you come on too strong when disciplining (i.e., grounding with removal of telephone, computer chatting, etc). A little goes a long way when it comes to this type of discipline for these kids. Time-outs can be effective for the younger child, as long as the parent is calm and consistent.

The Easy-Going Amiable: These people are nice, friendly, and relaxed. They are safety oriented and do not like upsetting people. They like harmony and will work hard to help others get along. They are good listeners and often make good counselors. They like people and tend to have a few close friends. They are accommodating and peace-seeking sometimes overempathizing or putting other's needs before their own. They like routine and are uncomfortable with change to their schedules or environment. They like to know *how* things are going to happen and *when*.

Amiables like everybody but are especially attracted to the energy and pep of Drivers and Expressives. They will often pair up for the long term with a Driver because they are the only ones willing to put up with the Driver's bossy, pointed attitude. Since confrontation leaves them feeling drained, shaky, and concerned about what was said, they often avoid it. As a result, the confrontation-loving Driver will sometimes get bored with the lack of enthusiasm the Amiable puts into a fight. An Amiable who is backed into a corner (especially when defending her young) will respond very strongly, shocking those who know her best.

Children with an Amiable personality are easy to get along with. They are not disruptive and try hard to do what they are asked. The challenge with these children is that they tend to be followers. If they are not taught good decision-making skills while they are young and still idolize their parents, they can easily be led down a wrong path as a teen. They do not like when people argue, and they can get very angry at a parent who publicly stands up for them (for example, calls the school to complain). They thrive on routine as well as predictability and get anxious about changes in their environment. Teaching these kids why it is important to stand up for their beliefs and helping them with the skills to do so is extremely important. They can take all the world's problems on their shoulders if we don't stop them.

These kids will benefit from being taught assertiveness, good decision making, flexibility, and anxiety-related coping skills. Most discipline tools work on these kids as they are bothered more by disappointing people than by anything extra we might hand out.

The Careful Analytical: This group is task-oriented like the Drivers; however, they are focused on having the task done correctly—in fact, perfectly. They are very organized and patient (since perfection is a slow process) and will take all the time they need to do something right. They like order and think things through in a logical, critical way. Facts are more important to them than people, and they often enjoy working on their own.

They are not friendly or aggressive and usually have just one or two really close friends. They focus on the big picture and comply with the rules simply because that is the logical thing to do. They do not show their feelings easily and can be judgmental of others. These people can easily become loners and sometimes forget to eat or sleep when involved in a project. The Drivers make them crazy because of their disregard for detail and their rush to finish the task. Analyticals are often attracted to Expressives (sometimes wishing they were more like them) and will often wind up in a relationship with them.

Children in this category will like things set up in a precise fashion. They will organize their dresser, bedroom, and desk to reflect order and logical correctness. Disorganization drives them crazy and they might offer to clean something up as a fun afternoon of activity. Parents are often concerned over their reclusive nature and might try to force them to be more outgoing. Many social skills do not come naturally to this group (except in a very logical way), so some teaching in this area will be important.

These kids will need time to think when asked a question and should not be rushed into answering. They need to know *why* and *how* things are done. They will benefit from belonging to clubs (Mad Science, 4-H, Scouts), although be sure it is something they enjoy doing. Tact doesn't come naturally to them, and they often need help with empathy and compassion. Learning to get dirty and have fun can also be helpful for this child, but only if she is a willing participant.

For discipline, consequences work well with this group as long as there is a logical connection to the misbehaviour (a toy removed after throwing it at a sibling). If you try to remove something unrelated (no movie tonight because child threw a toy) the child will rebel and not learn anything useful. Because this personality enjoys time alone, grounding and time-outs are rarely effective and can be frustrating for the parent.

Being aware of our dominant personality traits and how they complement or contrast with our child's can be very useful. Two Drivers will argue often and love every minute of it. When a parent recognizes this and ensures the fights don't get personal, he can sit back and enjoy the competition. On the other hand, when a Driver parent has an Amiable child, these battles will be draining or possibly scary for the child and can be damaging to her self-esteem. Parents with an Expressive or Driver child will create extra struggle if they use controlling language, and an Expressive with an Analytical child may wonder if they come from different planets.

On a personal level, once a person is aware of their dominant tendencies it becomes easier to learn how to moderate certain behaviours. A Driver can learn to take other people's feelings into account and practice patience. An Expressive can learn to be more organized and to arrive on time. Amiables can be trained to be assertive and accept that some disagreement is healthy and inevitable. Analyticals can learn to be more spontaneous and to strive for good quality instead of perfection. Our personality does not change when we do this but rather becomes educated. Our natural behaviours will still resurface during a crisis, but at least we will be able to understand and grant forgiveness to both ourselves and our family when this happens.

> *FREE Parenting Tip: Learning about our child's personality and how it complements or contradicts our own can help us develop realistic expectations. Understanding that our discipline tools will work better with some personality styles than others will make our job easier and help us be more effective.*

From Learning to Love

Although our personality tends to have the greatest influence on how we behave, there are numerous other qualities that affect our daily lives. Becoming familiar with some of these categories makes it easier to accept differences and overcome obstacles with our loved ones.

Three such areas include our communication style, love language, and learning style. Because the categories for each of these areas share some labels, it can be hard to keep them separate in our minds. What's important is that we are able to recognize which categories seem to have the greatest influence on our children rather than worrying too much about which label to use.

As you read through the following descriptions, look for pieces that fit you and your family members and use that information to understand each other better. Just be careful not to put someone in a category and then refuse to allow him or her to change, as people might move between categories as they grow and develop.

The Way We Talk

Communication styles influence how fast a person talks and provide us with insight on how we can best connect with each other. Sometimes these categories blend in a person and other times they are totally separate. I've provided a very short summary of the categories, but a more complete understanding of this topic can be found by researching NLP Communication Styles.

Visual: People dominant in this style of communication will speak at a very fast pace, making many of us strain to keep up with them. They tend to be well organized and meticulously dressed and will sit or stand with their heads or bodies erect. They notice everything and will be first to recognize a change in appearance. They can often be heard saying things like "Is that clear?"; "Get the picture?"; "How does that look to you?" A visual learner does best with written instructions, especially when learning something challenging.

Auditory: These people are listeners and speak clearly at a moderate pace and volume. They choose their words carefully and like to hear themselves talk. They are easily distracted by noise and learn best by listening. Phrases they use are: "How does that sound?"; "Do you hear what I'm saying?" In learning, they memorize by steps, procedures, or sequences and will often be heard speaking their instructions aloud.

Kinesthetic: These slow, steady speakers can drive others crazy by refusing to speed up their speech. They like to touch and will often sit or stand closer to you than others. They say things like: "Keep in touch"; "I need to get a handle on this"; "How do you feel about that?" A kinesthetic learner will benefit by being allowed to sit on something that rolls, rocks, or has some other gentle movement when he is trying to learn something.

Digital: This group is about connecting, and I like to think of them as people who are strengthened by *plugging in* to others. They are similar to Auditories and have a moderate speech structure and pace. They have a strong need to feel like they are understood and have a very active chatterbox in their head. *Why* is a common question for this group since they need to understand things in order to learn them. They also say things like: "Does that make sense?"; "Are you with me?"; "Are we connecting here?"

Knowing where our families fit into these categories can help us understand things better when problems arise. For example, a child who is a visual or auditory learner will have an easier time at school than the child who is kinesthetic and needs to move around to process instructions. If he is also a kinesthetic communicator, he might be pushed to talk faster and corrected for sitting too close to others. As a result, this child can go through school feeling frustrated, unfocused, and socially rejected unless his parents or teacher understand him and work to accommodate his needs.

The Way We Love

Our love languages[9] determine the way we receive love easiest and will be our first choice for how we send love to others. Becoming aware of our family's primary love languages can be both helpful and rewarding.

A word of warning … Although most of the category names are the same as those used in communication and learning, they do not need to match. For example, a person can be an auditory communicator, a kinesthetic learner, and have a visual primary love language. Although this might seem confusing, it is part of what makes us unique.

A person whose primary love language is visual will feel most loved when she receives things she can see: gifts, love notes, a clean house, or a thoughtful dinner on the table. Coming home to a messy house or receiving nothing for important life milestones can be very upsetting.

Auditories need to *hear* that you love them. They feel most loved when hearing words of affirmation like: "I love you"; "You look great"; and "I love spending time with you." They will do well in any relationship that shares verbal praise and encouragement. A disapproving tone of voice or set of words can be very upsetting to them.

The kinesthetics, or *touchers,* in the crowd will require physical contact like hand-holding, hugs, fingers running through their hair, or gentle massage. A joking push or a shrugging off of their hand can be taken as serious rejection.

---

9   **Chapman, Gary D.,** *The Five Love Languages: How to Express Heartfelt Commitment to Your Mate* **(Chicago, IL: Northfield Publishing, 2004).**

The digital *connectors* respond well to shared laughter, meaningful conversation, and quality time together and can be quite bothered if not asked about how they are doing or what they were up to that day.

Learning which love languages your family falls into can help you determine where to put your energy when it comes to showing love. For example, imagine you receive love best visually (notes, flowers, etc.) but your partner is putting all his energy into telling you how much he cares. This suggests his primary love language is auditory, yet you put all your effort into leaving notes on his pillow, sending love email, and other visual cues. Both of you are putting time and energy into growing the love in your relationship. Both of you are working far harder than you'd have to if you used the right language.

The Way We Learn

The environment we learn in is also important and unique for each of us. A lot of relationship-damaging arguments with our kids occur over homework and the environment it should be done in. Understanding and supporting our child's needs will help him become confident in his ability and promote harmony in the home.

According to the Dunn and Dunn Learning Styles Model, there are at least twenty-one variables that influence how each of us learn best. Becoming aware of these variables and working with our child to figure out which ones work best for him can be quite eye-opening.

Some of the factors that are important in learning environments are surprising.

- **Lighting.** Some of us learn better with the lighting turned low and find it hard to concentrate with bright lights shining on our paper. This seems like something our parents warned us against, yet bright light is not always the answer.

- **Noise.** A quiet library environment is what most of us picture as the ideal learning environment, but that's not always best. Some people actually require background noise like music or a television to learn optimally.

- **Eating and Drinking.** Eating food or sipping on a drink are not activities most of us think of as having anything to do with learning. But for some children, this sort of intake really helps. Knowing this is the case for a child can help us be understanding and help the child to learn.

- **Environment.** The space, temperature, and design of the room can affect how easy or hard it is for a child to learn, with some doing better with warmth or sprawled on a couch. Many of us see the sprawl as lazy and unfocused, yet for our kids it could be the key to success.

> *FREE Parenting Tip: There are qualities about each of us that influence how we learn, love, and communicate. When we make the effort to understand each other, we are much more tolerant of our differences and have a greater chance of getting our message across.*

If we are not aware of the kinds of things that make it easier for our kids to learn, it will be challenging for us to support them. It is common for parents to try to push their preferred learning environment onto their child, thinking they are doing the right thing. To really help our child, we need to first understand him and then allow him to be that wonderful, unique individual.

From learning, to love, to communication, we are all different. Allowing others to express themselves in their own unique way speaks volumes; we just have to make sure we are tuning in to their station.

Exercise: Creating the Family You Want

Learning why we do the things we do and what makes each of us tick can be a lifelong process. Use this exercise to help you get to know your family better and then continue to update and change as needed.

Family of Origin

Are there things from your family of origin that you are doing with your kids and would like to stop? If so, write them here along with a note about when you tend to use them and what you might do instead. If you are working with a partner, compare your charts and discuss.

For example: lots of rules; look at rules and keep only those that I have good reason for.

Strategies to work on:

_____

_____

_____

_____

_____

_____

Put a check beside the lines that best describe the family you were raised in. Use the extra lines to write down other tools or descriptive statements you feel are relevant:

____ many strict rules	____ few to no rules
____ consequences strongly enforced	____ no consequences or not enforced
____ harsh punishments	____ punishment sporadic
____ little to no discussion or negotiation	____ lots of guilt
____ outside involvement discouraged	____ no family enforcer or varied
____ one main enforcer in family	____ love conditional on behaviour
____ love rarely spoken of or shown	____ accusations of "not caring" common
____ put-downs/attacking statements common	____ threats common but rarely carried out
____ lots of threats	____ lots of discussion but nothing decided
____ fear a common feeling	____ confusion or frustration a common feeling
____ a few clear rules	_____
____ consequences carried out consistently	_____
____ variety of discipline tools used	_____
____ no harsh punishments	_____
____ discussions, negotiation, compromise common	_____
____ love given unconditionally	_____
____ mutual respect built	_____
____ putdowns or insults rare if ever	_____
____ threats rare	_____
____ fear or confusion uncommon	_____

It can also be helpful to create a profile for each person in your family. Write down whatever fits for personality, communication mode, love language, and learning environment information. Then note the suggestions that might help you really connect with them or help them to grow. You might need to do some experimenting to really understand their unique style of being. Please remember that all styles and modes are good and perfectly acceptable.

For example:

Debbie
Personality: *Amiable with some Analytical and Driver pieces*
Communication Mode: *Auditory, Digital*
Love Language: *Digital, Auditory*
Learning Environment: *Daylight or soft lighting, tea/water beside, desk, warm, quiet*

Might need to be taught how to be assertive and how to let go of perfectionism. She dislikes arguing but likes changes in routine. Discipline that shows her what she did wrong and why it's a problem will work well—letting her know how she disappointed others will be enough. She communicates best when given verbal instruction but needs to understand why something must be done. She feels most loved when people try to connect with her and give verbal praise or feedback.

Name: _____

Personality Type: _____

Communication Mode: _____

Love Language: _____

Preferred Learning Environment: _____

Tips to help me connect with this person:

_____

_____

_____

_____

_____

_____

_____

Chapter 6: A Powerful Topic

My Bathtime Trials

Bathtime with my kids provided me with more opportunity to practice parenting skills than any other activity. Both of my kids resisted getting into the bath from the beginning, no matter how fun or enticing I tried to make it. At first, I took it personally and decided I must be doing something wrong. It didn't help that all my friends' kids seemed to love their baths and would even ask to take one for enjoyment.

After a while, I realized that while my kids had started out with fairly common resistance, I had let it turn into a power struggle and had created a problem that was much bigger than it needed to be. Sharing the things I tried to make bathtime work in our house might be helpful or at least enjoyable for other parents to read. Here are some of the things I tried:

Making it fun: I bought all kinds of bath toys, stickers, foams, and other items to make bathtime fun and exciting. Once the kids were in the bath, they could stay there for hours and never run out of things to do. Unfortunately, my challenge was in getting my kids *into* the tub, not keeping them in there, so this solution did not really solve my problem.

Reasoning: I would always start out trying to gain compliance from my child in a cheerful and friendly manner. I would explain why baths were important, that they didn't want to stink, and that even parents have to bathe. Any explanation longer than four words made them lose interest, but sometimes they gave in.

Logical consequences: I tried telling them that dirty kids are smelly kids and no one wants to snuggle with a smelly child (natural/logical consequence). The problem was when snuggle time came around and they hadn't had a bath, I couldn't possibly reinforce my earlier warning. Putting them to bed without snuggling during story time was impossible for me.

Choices: Do you want to have your bath before supper or after? Would you like to have a bath or a shower? Do you want to bring the basket of toys or some from your room? I tried all kinds of choices. Sometimes they worked, but usually my daughter's response to every choice was, "No bath!"

Reverse Psychology: "You don't want to have a bath. That would make you clean and you wouldn't want that. You can't possibly beat me to the bathtub." I thought maybe I could confuse them by telling them they didn't want to have a bath, but they simply agreed with me.

Threats/Brute Strength: When my kids were really little, I calmly continued with bathtime despite their cries of protest. I was gentle but firm and simply put them in the tub. As they got bigger, this did not work, as kids can stop the descent into the tub no matter how hard you try to hold all their limbs together in one package. That moved me to threatening, "Get in that tub, right now!" This took far too much energy, rarely worked, and I never felt good doing it.

Letting Them Drive: After many successful and unsuccessful strategies for getting my kids to bathe, I gave up and let them decide how often they got in the tub. I would tell them if they were smelly or if their hair looked greasy, but, in the end, the decision was up to them.

I'm happy to report that, as teenagers, both kids are regular with their showers and put time and effort into their self-care. Had I backed off when they were younger, they might have had less reason to resist, and this struggle could have ended much sooner. On the other hand, they might have still resisted and become the dirtiest, smelliest kids around.

Understanding Our Response-Ability

The way we parent, the things we enforce, and the way we enforce them, should all complement our job description of parenting. If, for example, we want our children to learn *how* to think, we need to give them opportunities to figure things out. If we tell them *what* to think instead, "You will do it because I told you to and I'm your parent," we are not being consistent with our goals.

One of the biggest concerns I have with our societal message for children today is the inconsistent message we give in the area of responsibility. By having laws that allow people to blame others for their mistakes or accidents, we are teaching that responsibility for our actions lies outside of ourselves. For example, if I was to go to your place and slip on your wet floor, it is not your fault that I fell down. Fault does not lie with the company that made my shoes, the people who made the flooring, or Mother Nature for providing the water. I fell down. If anyone has to take responsibility for that, it's me. "But accidents happen, it's nobody's fault," you might say. So let's look at another example.

Let's say I'm twelve years old and my parents drop me off at a store for an hour to hang out with a couple of friends. A half hour later, my parents are called and told I'm in the security department having been caught shoplifting. Is that my parents' fault for trusting me on my own for an hour? Is it my friends' fault since they have a history of bad behaviour and obviously led me astray? Is it the store's fault for having so many lovely things out there that I could take? No. It is my fault for stealing.

Unfortunately, our society likes to blame the parents, and often the parents will transfer the blame to someone else (for instance, my friends). When this happens, I learn that my bad choice is actually outside of my control and therefore not my fault. Our legal system and our current way of thinking are set up to teach our children they do not need to take responsibility for their actions. It is also set up to cause many parents to distrust their children and fear their child making a mistake.

We can teach our kids how to take responsibility for their own behaviour by practicing the following:

- **Model responsibility taking.** When our kids hear us talking about someone who *made us so mad we lost it; the traffic that made us late;* or *how we wouldn't have backed over her bike if she hadn't left it out*, they are learning how to put off responsibility. It is partly the child's fault that her bike got run over, but accepting our part in the accident will teach a child far more than any finger-pointing.

For example: "I'm so sorry I ran over your bike, I really wish it hadn't been behind my car."

- **Let bygones be bygones.** Sometimes it is important to know what led up to the situation at hand … other times not so much. Whenever possible put your focus on what has happened and what can be done to fix it rather than harshly asking for a reason. When you must get more information, do it as respectfully and non-judgmentally as possible.[10]

  For example: "I'm really disappointed my lamp is broken. What's our rule about throwing things in the house?"

- **Focus on your child's role in the situation.** When our kids come up with a reason they are not responsible for something that went wrong and we shift our focus with them, we are rewarding them for not taking responsibility. Even if it was the neighbor boy who threw the rock at the window, we are best off to acknowledge this information and return to our child's involvement in the situation.

  For example: "I understand Jack was the one who threw the rock, now let's talk about what you're going to do to make up for your part in breaking Mr. Jones window."

We need to teach our children, starting from a very young age, to take responsibility for what they have done. If we believe mistakes are

---

10   Chapter 11 provides communication ideas to avoid putting our kids on the defensive.

an opportunity to learn and grow, then taking responsibility for an error is not a bad thing.

Response-Ability Lies within Us

Have you ever noticed that two (or more) people can be in exactly the same situation, yet respond in a totally different way? This is because there is a gap between the incident and how they respond to that incident. This gap provides an opportunity for us to choose how we will respond in any situation.[11] Sometimes that gap feels so small that it seems as if our response was automatic and therefore outside of our control, but this is never the case.

When something happens to us (stimulus), there is always an opportunity (gap) for us to choose how we will react (response).

$$Stimulus{\rightarrow}Gap{\rightarrow}Response$$

This is important for us to understand and to teach to our children. If someone does something and we feel angry, our body is signaling us that something might be wrong.[12] The stimulus (what that person said) did not cause our anger; the stimulus or event is always neutral. The same comment that made you angry might make another person smile or feel nothing at all. There is nothing right or wrong about the feeling we have in response; it is what we do with that signal that can cause a problem. So, no matter how it might seem, that person did not create our feeling, something in us did.

---

11   Covey, Stephen, *The 7 Habits of Highly Effective Families* (New York: Golden Books, 1997) p. 27.

12   Potter-Efron, Ron, *Angry All the Time: An Emergency Guide to Anger Control* (Oakland, CA: New Harbinger, 1994) p. 3.

When a strong emotion like anger shoots through us, it is hard to find the gap and take advantage of the opportunity it provides. When I am working with students, I like to teach them a simple word (for example, "Whoa!") to throw into that gap when they are emotionally upset. This increases the size of the gap and provides them more time to come up with their response. Some people find it easier to shift their focus to a part of their body (for example, their feet) rather than use a word. Any trick that helps them stop the flood of emotion so they can think more clearly is beneficial. The gap is always there, we just have to use it.

Once a person has mastered recognizing this gap, he is now in a position to choose his response. Sometimes he will choose badly, but at least he did it with awareness. What's important is that he understands he chose his response and now needs to take responsibility for it. Once responsibility is accepted, there is plenty of learning that can take place, but without it nothing good can happen.

Crooked thinking (believing others are to blame for your actions) allows people to bully, abuse, and engage in other hurtful behaviours. It is our job as parents to help our children recognize that their actions always belong to them. By taking control of our own actions, especially when we'd rather blame others, we are taking advantage of the gap and role-modeling true response-ability.

FREE Parenting Tip: Our children need to take responsibility for their actions and we need to show them how. Being aware of the gap that allows us to choose our own response helps with this task.

Introducing Parent Power

Children are born with very little power and rely on us to dress them, feed them, bathe them, and put them to bed. If our baby refuses to eat or sleep we understand that we cannot force him to comply, so we try different food, shuffle the sleeping schedule, and do everything we can to get him working with us.

As our children get older and more verbal, some of us begin to lose our willingness to see it their way and start to insist they comply with our wishes. They continue to develop stronger opinions, and we become more and more determined to have it our way. Most times, we truly believe that what we are enforcing is necessary for our child's safety, health, or well-being. Other times, we know we are enforcing it because we are tired, irritated, embarrassed, or otherwise bothered.

Parent Power refers to the authority given to us as parents to enforce rules and boundaries with our children in order to teach them right from wrong. When it comes to an impasse, in which our child simply won't see our side of the message and we aren't willing (or able) to go with his, Parent Power is what we use to get our way. It is about having the final word and is probably where statements like "Because I said so," or "As long as you're under my roof" came from. It relies on our children believing in our authority for it to work and is given to us based on the trust condition that we will use it appropriately. Unfortunately, there is plenty of opportunity to misuse Parent Power since it is basically unmonitored and we're not taught how to use it wisely.

The trick with Parent Power is that it must be used by a calm, controlled parent. Used wisely it helps us guide our children in making decisions, showing them we have their best interests at heart and earning their respect. This is important because as our children grow, their power increases until eventually we find ourselves relying on the respect we have built with them to gain cooperation. If we haven't used the early years to build this respect, things can get extremely challenging when our kids get older.

Used positively, Parent Power is a backup to be used after other tools have failed. To illustrate, let's pretend you ask your young daughter to come and clean up her crafts. She ignores you and sits down at the computer getting ready to play. You walk over, place your hand calmly across the keyboard, and assertively tell her, "I've asked you to clean up your crafts. Do that first please." She starts to whine and fuss insisting you remove your hand and saying she'll clean up later. Remaining calm, you give her an option, such as "Clean up your crafts before playing on the computer or the computer is off for the day and you can go to your room while I clean up your crafts." She doesn't listen and angrily begins tugging at your hand. You pick her up and carry her to her room calmly but firmly telling her she must stay there until she has calmed down and is ready to listen. In this situation, you have modeled assertiveness and options statements before using your Parent Power to enforce your instruction.

The problem with Parent Power arises when we skip the learning piece and jump straight into getting our way. In other words, we ask (or demand) our child clean up her crafts and when she doesn't listen we *make* her do it. "That's it! You're off the computer for today and maybe longer if you don't smarten up. Clean up your mess, now!"

To illustrate this point further here's an example many of us can relate to. Imagine you are driving to an appointment and are behind schedule. Your kids are coming with you (although they don't want to) and are arguing in the back seat. Shooting them your I-mean-business look in the mirror, you growl, "If I have to stop this car …!"

At this point, things can go a couple of different ways. One thing that could happen, ideally, is the misbehaviour stops. The kids understand the implied threat, are unsure what will happen if the car is pulled over, and are not willing to take a chance and find out. Your power has effectively worked, although your kids have not learned anything useful and won't know how to apply this information to their next argument.

Another thing that could happen is that the kids continue to misbehave, creating a serious problem. You've put out a threat that implies something bad will happen if you stop the car, and now you have to follow-through. What the heck are you going to do? You're already late, the kids would be happy not to have to go, and you have no plan for what you are going to do once the car is stopped!

In this situation, most parents will repeat the threat or start throwing out other consequences rather than actually following through and stopping the car. "Just wait until we get home! You guys probably think you're still going to a movie on the weekend." If this happens, the kids have just called your bluff and have learned to challenge your threats in the future.

Of course, some parents will be so angry they will pull the car over and proceed to act. The problem is now the parent feels threatened (we hate having our power questioned), angry, and is late for her appointment. Overreaction is quite probable, which, if it involves brute force could be crossing the line to abuse, a place where most of us would never willingly go.

Any time we overreact and "lose it" we diminish our Parent Power. It is very difficult to respect a person who lacks self-control and uses her power unfairly. In fact, when we see other adults behave this way, our respect for them lessens.

Knowing that we have this power and saving it for those times when we really need it allows us to work on building respect rather than forcing compliance. Our power is a gift. We should use it wisely.

> *FREE Parenting Tip: If we use our power to build respect and to guide our children, it will help us set a strong foundation for the years ahead. If we use our power only to get our way, it will cause us much grief and frustration. The choice is ours, and we do have the power to make a difference.*

A Force *Not* to Be Reckoned With

"I don't want to go to bed."
"You can't make me."
"I hate peas."
"No bath!"

These are typical assertions made by kids. They start when our kids recognize they have some control over things involving their body and stops when we recognize that too. A power struggle refers to any time two people disagree on something and are both determined to get their way. Power struggles are not about negotiating, discussing, or thinking things through—they are about using power to get our way.

Consider this example of a three-year-old who has had a full day of tiring play and a parent who is equally exhausted:

"Eat your supper," Mom says in an authoritative voice.

"No, not hungry," responds Taylor, crossing her arms and closing her mouth tightly.

"Eat it now or you are going to bed," Mom says, leaning across the table with a serious I-mean-business look.

"No, not go to bed, not hungry!" Taylor cries, laying her head in her arms on the table and sobbing.

"You're getting your hair in the supper. Sit up or you are in bed for the night!" Mom yells, standing up to her full height and quickly moving Taylor's plate out of the way of her hair.

Taylor flops to the floor kicking and screaming in full-blown tantrum. Mom picks her up, and, with Taylor's limbs flailing, carries her to her room. This story can be repeated for bath time, clean-up time, or bedtime, and can take anywhere from thirty seconds to a few hours to build.

Depending on the personalities of the people involved, this can begin to happen when the kids are very little. How we handle the situation can determine how often and for how long these incidents continue to occur.

When we engage in a power struggle, things can go only one of two ways.

1. We can win and thereby teach our children that as long as you're bigger, stronger, and louder you can get your way. As a result, they crave more power.

2. We can lose and allow our children to learn how powerful it feels to win a battle of the wills resulting in their craving more power.

Our kids have nothing to lose and much to gain by engaging in these struggles. We, on the other hand, have much to lose and little to gain.

So what can we do to avoid these struggles? Like most things in life, we prevent it by thinking ahead.

Here are six ways to prevent power struggles:

1. Be clear about your expectations and provide good reasons for your beliefs.

    "I believe my child needs to eat breakfast in the morning because that energy feeds his brain and his body and makes him better able to face the day."

2. Explain your expectations to your child. Don't make this a lengthy lecture but rather an age-appropriate explanation. If necessary, decide on a consequence for slip-ups or rewards for compliance.

    "Breakfast is an important part of our day, so I want to make sure you always have a good one. You may have a treat with lunch if you have a good breakfast."

3. Understand that your child wants to have some say over his life, and one of the few areas he can truly control is his body. Give him as much choice as possible. Have a list of foods you approve for breakfast (fruit, for one) and foods you don't (potato chips).

    "Do you want cereal or toast for breakfast?" or *"What would you like to have for breakfast?"*

4. Refuse to fight. When your child decides to flex his power muscle, focus your energy on self-control. We know it takes two to fight; we just don't like to believe we would fight with a five-year-old. Kids love to push our buttons—it's a very powerful feeling to make an adult flip out. Stay calm and clear about

your expectations, protect your anger button, and refuse to go to battle.

"Breakfast is one of our rules. Do you want to choose what you'll eat or should I?"

5. Be consistent. A rule worth having is a rule worth enforcing. On special occasions you can make changes, but overall the rule should be there for a valid reason and therefore be worth insisting on.

Calmly repeat your rule: *"Breakfast is an important part of our day."*

6. If you do engage in a power struggle, acknowledge it to your child (later) and assure him the rule is still in force.

"That fight we had over breakfast was wrong, and I'm sorry it happened. Breakfast is an important part of the day and is still a rule in our house."

Power struggles are a force not to be reckoned with, because we want our kids to feel empowered without the need for power over others.

FREE Parenting Tip: Most of us will be unable to avoid every power struggle, but if we can cut them down to occasional events, life will be easier. There will be days when we are deep into a struggle before we recognize what's happening. This is normal! What's important is that we recognize and learn from it. It takes two to tango. The question is, how badly do we want to dance?

Surviving a Power Struggle

Getting out of a power struggle without causing extra damage can be very challenging. This section is set up to help guide you out of this situation as gracefully as possible.

Let's assume you are immersed in a battle of wills with a child who is refusing to take her bath. She has no reason for not wanting to bathe other than she would rather play. You started out nice, moved on to authoritative, and are now angrily ready to force your way. This is a battle for power between an adult and a young child. It might be funny if you weren't so darn mad.

The first thing you must do is get control of yourself! Take a deep breath and remind yourself that tomorrow this will seem like a much smaller deal. If necessary, get away from the child so you can focus on calming down. Do not try to deal with the situation when you are emotionally stirred up.

If you have a partner who could help, call for backup—"I need time to calm down. Take over please." Then take a time-out in the bathroom, your bedroom, or some other place where you can be by yourself. You must calm down in order to get blood flowing to the thinking area of your brain. This is not about asking your partner to take over the battle. Although he might be willing to do so, if he does this on a regular basis, it can become frustrating for all parties and can make things much harder for you when he is not there.

If help is not available, remove yourself as best you can from the situation while still looking after your responsibilities. For example, if you have a baby as well as the child you're fighting with, put your baby in his crib/playpen with a toy or bring him with you wherever you are going. Another possibility is to put the child you are fighting with in her room, shut the door, and tell her you both need a time-out to calm down. Another option is to call a friend, neighbor, or family member to come and help out for an hour or so.

Once you have calmed down, think about your next step. Try to put things in perspective. Your overall relationship with your child is more important than getting your way at all costs. Search for any humor in the situation, assess where you are at, and think about where you need to go next.

Now That You're Calm, Let's Deal with the Storm

FREE Parenting Tip: It is harder to deal with things in the heat of the moment. Anticipating problems in advance and creating a plan for what you can do will decrease battle wounds and make recovery that much quicker.

If your struggle was about something you do not have a plan for, it's time to develop one (not right this moment, but within the next couple days). This will involve coming up with your expectations, having an age-appropriate discussion with your child, determining any consequences or rewards, and putting the plan into place. For now, you might tell your child, "I guess bathtime needs a plan. Let's do that tomorrow right after supper." If you've already set up rules on this topic, figure out which to apply and calmly put them in place.

You might still want the child to have a bath tonight, but you'll need to be very careful about not reengaging in the battle. Visualize different ways you could say things to your child before saying it to her aloud so that unfair choices can be made more appealing—for example, "Do you want to take your bath willingly or am I going to have to force you?" might become, "I need you to take a bath tonight. What can I do to help make that happen?"

If your child has calmed down and you already have a plan, you might say something like, "I'm sorry I yelled at you—that was wrong. We agreed you would take a bath once a week, and tonight is the night. If we move fast, we can get your bath done and still have a few minutes left for stories."

If she is still upset, give her more time. There is no use having a discussion until you are both calm enough to think. "I can see you're still upset. I'll give you more time to calm down." An out-of-control child needs to learn that only she can control her responses.

If you are calm and she is still escalating, she needs time to pull it together. Sometimes that means focusing on something else and ignoring her. Other times it means getting her safely into her room or giving her a hug (if she wants one). I found humming or singing quietly while pretending to ignore my child had a calming effect on us both.

If she is so upset that your struggle moves into bedtime, put her to bed and tell her you will do the bath the next day. "It's gotten too late for your bath. Let's get you to bed, and we'll do bath first thing when I get home from work tomorrow."

Start early the next day so you have room to move without running into bedtime again. It is essential that you follow-through the next day. By staying calm you are sending a message that this is non-negotiable and she might as well comply.

Photocopy the following (or write it out yourself) and post it on your fridge as a helpful reminder to get you out of the battle zone.

In Case of a Power Struggle—Emergency Guidelines

Calm down

This is a learning experience for both of us

Be clear and consistent

Breathe in deeply through my nose feeling the air go all the way down to my toes

Focus on the bottoms of my feet

Exhale slowly feeling the tension in my muscles leave with my exhale

Breathe again

Feel my feet still firmly in place

Remember, an out-of-control child needs an in-control adult

Help my child regain self-control

Give her space, hum quietly, hug him, whatever will be helpful and accepted

When we are both calm, be consistent and follow-through with my rule

If my requests are reasonable, calmly persevere until my child complies

Apologize if I have done or said things that model bad behaviour

Use positive language and tone of voice to recognize my child's need for power

Exercise: The Game of Blame

When we allow our children to blame other people or things for something that has happened to them, we disempower them. Power is gained by having a perceived sense of control in a situation. The only thing any of us can truly control is ourselves. If we do not accept responsibility for our role in the things we have done, we end up feeling disempowered and miserable. If we teach our kids to accept responsibility for their actions and to forgive both themselves and others for mistakes, we have given them an ability to use their power for good.

Read the following story and answer the questions below:

One day you are walking down the sidewalk when a boy on a skateboard zooms in front of you forcing you to jump to the side. The edge of the sidewalk crumbles as you step onto it, causing your foot to slip off and your ankle to break. In extreme pain, you are brought to the hospital and end up with a cast and a bottle full of painkillers. That night you suffer from severe chest pains as well as throbbing up and down your injured leg. You return to the hospital to learn a reaction to the painkiller is causing intense swelling and heart palpitations. A nurse informs you confidentially that a number of people have had negative reactions to this painkiller, but it is still on the market. Your heart is stabilized and you are given a new drug and sent home with your cast still painfully in place. After seven days of occasional chest pains and discomfort radiating from your foot, you return to the hospital. X-rays show the ankle bone shifted when the cast was put on causing your ankle to heal incorrectly. It needs to be rebroken. Your blood pressure is through the roof, and they are concerned there might be permanent damage to your heart.

Write a list of all the people who might be considered at fault for your current situation.

_____

_____

_____

_____

What would be the benefit of blaming any of these people?
For example: *the drug company; benefit = gets drug off the market*

_____

_____

_____

_____

Jot down how blaming any of the above would help your body heal.

_____

_____

_____

_____

In reality, playing the game of blame will not help you in any way. Your focus needs to be on healing. Some might argue that the drug company needs to be taken to task so the drug is removed from the market; that the doctor is negligent for using this drug and putting the cast on wrong; or that the skateboarder should be fined for being on the sidewalk. My question is how do these actions help you heal or move on in your life?

Blaming others traps energy in a negative cycle and refuses to let you move on. In this case it can challenge your immune system, cause extra stress, and interfere with the healing process. In other cases, it can stop you from really living your life. It can destroy relationships, affect your work, and make you bitter. Blaming weakens us and leaves us feeling powerless. We need to hold tight to our power and focus on what is within our control. Forgiving others for their possible role in our plight is a gift we can give ourselves.

Once you're healed, you might decide to check out what's happening with the sidewalk, the doctor, or the drug company. You might write letters or do some research in these areas. If you do, make sure it is to inform, not to blame.

That's the game of blame. You may choose to play it. In fact, it might be what gives you a reason to get up in the morning. If so, use it to help you, then when you are ready to heal, let go of the blame and allow positive energy to fill in its space.

Chapter 7: Creating Structure and Control

My Clothing Concerns

As my kids were growing up, we went through a variety of struggles around clothing. I tried really hard to let go and allow them to wear whatever they wanted, but it was quite difficult. One of the things that saved me during those years was reading Barbara Coloroso's book *Kids Are Worth It!* and discovering her idea of creating an "I dressed myself!" pin for kids to wear.[13] I never actually made a pin, but it made me feel better to know I wasn't the only parent with a strangely dressed child.

There was one year when my child wore the same T-shirt for the first half of the school year and a second T-shirt every day for the second half. On Sunday, I'd have to wrestle the shirt off to wash it so it could be back and ready to go for Monday.

---

13   Coloroso, Barbara, *Kids Are Worth It! Giving Your Child the Gift of Inner Discipline* (**Toronto, ON: Somerville House, 1995**) **p. 76.**

My other child gained comfort from old, worn-out clothing and wouldn't let me get rid of anything ripped, stained, or otherwise. I tried to make these "playclothes only," but somehow they would end up being worn whenever my child was nervous. Buying new clothing to wear for a Santa picture was definitely a waste of money.

The one thing I didn't struggle with when my kids were young was about dressing warm enough. We live in Manitoba, Canada, where it can get cold enough to freeze body parts off, so dressing warm is part of our survival. When the kids were little and looked underdressed, I'd tell them to go stand out on our deck and see if they were warm enough. If they could stay out there for five minutes and be warm enough, they could go out in what they had on. Inevitably, they would come in after a minute and add clothes to their body on these occasions.

There was a time when my son was around nine that he decided he didn't need a winter jacket despite the below-freezing temperatures. I tried a variety of things to convince him he needed his jacket, but he kept telling me he was warm enough. I had raised both of my kids to listen to their body, so this really stumped me. Finally, I told him his thermostat must be broken if he thought he was warm enough and, until it was fixed, I would need to decide his outdoor gear. That worked, and he dressed sensibly—until he became a teenager.

Practicing Self-Control

Self-control is a learned behaviour that requires both social and emotional skill development. It is easier for us to maintain self-control in the public eye although some people "let it fly" regardless of their audience. Over time, losing self-control in public has become more common, with horrific examples being displayed in the media and movies on a regular basis. As a result, most of us witness people losing self-control often which desensitizes us, making it seem normal and acceptable.

Many parents struggle to model and teach this skill since they were never taught it themselves. They figured out how to use their self-control to avoid unpleasant alternatives like spankings, the strap, imprisonment, etc. As a result, they do not know how to effectively teach this life skill, and their kids are growing up without it.

Stress seems to play a role in both the intensity and the frequency that people lose their self-control. Between aging parents, demanding jobs, financial concerns, illnesses, and relationship difficulties, stress does appear to be on the rise for many people. Since it's not socially appropriate to snap at a client, colleague, or grocery clerk, many of us hold it in and take it home with us. We don't do this on purpose—it's just that when we get home and take off our *public face* the guard is released on both our pent-up emotions and our social behaviours. Our children misbehave and snap—we lose it. The more we allow ourselves to lose our self-control the easier it becomes to do it again.

There are three things to keep in mind if we want to be successful in both learning and teaching self-control:

1. We must become self-aware so we can pick up on cues early and take action before a major reaction occurs.

2. We must practice new behaviours and create new patterns to follow. In times of stress we take the path we are most familiar with, making our patterns repeat.[14]

3. We must have a real desire to succeed. Just saying we wish we were more controlled will not make it happen. We have to truly want it or our negative thoughts will overpower our optimistic ones.

If we understand and accept these three points, then there are plenty of things we can do to maintain our control. What we do on a regular basis to deal with stress and challenges in our life will influence how easy it is for us to lose it. Putting into action the following practices on a regular basis is beneficial in many ways.

Positive Thinking: Our thoughts have the greatest influence on our being calm and staying in control or, alternatively, on feeding the fire and losing it. By controlling our thoughts we control our actions. Having a number of simple phrases we can silently recite when we feel our emotions taking over is a critical part of regaining control. Coming up with those ideas in the heat of the moment is nearly impossible to do, so it makes sense to create some ideas when we are relaxed and in control. Examples of such phrases might be: "Calm down"; "I'm okay"; "Relax"; "Whoa"; "I can handle this"; "It's not worth a fight." You must allow your feelings to change with these thoughts or an over-reaction is still likely to occur.

---

14   Robbins, Anthony, *Personal Power II* (**San Diego, CA: Robbins Research International, 1966) vol. 2, cassette 1.**

Breathing: Our breathing greatly affects how we feel. By focusing on our breathing and taking deep breaths, we can help our bodies relax and take a moment to refocus our thinking. Some people like to combine counting with their breathing and others just like to focus on the breath itself. See which works for you and practice in times of calm.

Exercise: When we are carrying around a lot of extra emotion and stress, exercise can be a great way to work it off. Exercise does not fix unrelated problems, but the benefits go beyond self-control and it can be a great way to work off some steam. Try to work positive thoughts (from the earlier positive thinking example) into your workout for the greatest effect.

Relaxation: Our goal when we are feeling stressed is to help the body relax and release tension. This can be done using stretches, yoga, breath work, or any variety of relaxation techniques. Some people like to fill their body up like a balloon and then let the breath and tension out in a big rush. Others prefer to breathe slowly and focus on releasing the tension out of their body piece by piece. It's great to know which works best for you so you can use it at a moments notice.

FREE Parenting Tip: Many people rebalance by going for a walk, sitting under a tree, patting a dog, or watching a fish tank. Nature has a calm way of being that will transfer to us if allowed. Concrete, electromagnetic fields, and satellite signals all take their toll on our bodies. Mother Nature provides wonderful examples of living in the moment, if we can find the time to notice.

Regaining Control in the Heat of the Moment

While all of the earlier ideas can help us find balance, not all of them will help in the heat of the moment. Here are some ideas to help when tough situations arise or to teach self-control to a child who struggles.

Focus on the bottoms of the feet. If you find you are getting emotional and need something quick to divert your center of attention, try focusing on the bottoms of your feet. Really feel them stuck to the floor and notice where there is pressure. This does two things: it grounds you by tuning you in to the physical, and it tells the brain there is no emergency, allowing blood to flow back to the thinking part of your brain.

Breathe in a box. Picture a box in your head and breathe around its borders—up one side, across the top, down the other side, and across the bottom. This translates into: breathe in for four, hold for four, breathe out for four, and think positive thoughts for four. If you picture a box while you are doing this, you will again refocus your brain from its emergency state.

Bite your tongue. Most of us have heard this "advice" before, but few of us have ever actually followed it. The act of allowing angry words to shoot out of your mouth actually escalates your emotion. If you can hold your tongue with your teeth and your mouth firmly shut while focusing on positive thoughts, your emotions will cool and you will hear things you would have otherwise missed.

Scratch the record.[15] Our lives are full of patterns that put us on autopilot so we do not need to constantly think about what we are doing. It is common for people to get into emotional ruts, which cause them to get caught in a loop and repeat undesirable behaviour. If we imagine these patterns as grooves on a record (or CD), all we need to do is scratch the record to interrupt them. You can do this by surprising yourself, making a funny face, shouting out a goofy word ("Kowabunga!"), or jumping up and down—anything out of the ordinary for you.[16]

Identify the cause. Often what seems like the obvious reason for our anger isn't the cause at all. If we can make ourselves focus objectively on why we are so angry, our brain shifts out of fight mode and into analysis mode, calming our emotions and allowing us to think. We might ask aloud, "What is going on? Why am I so angry about this?" This causes our brain to search for an answer and might provide our sparring partner time to do a self check as well. Of course, if we are focused on blaming and negativity, our brain will supply the information we are requesting. A true analyst would remove emotion and look for facts.

Protect your button. We become defensive when we feel under attack. If we refuse to take things personally and focus on protecting our anger button, we can have some fun instead of overreacting. This sounds easy but it's not. For example, as mentioned in Chapter 4, we

---

15   Robbins, Anthony. *Personal Power II* (San Diego, CA: Robbins Research International, 1966) vol. 2, cassette 2.

16   These are not things you would do on the bus or in a meeting, but when it comes to dealing with your kids in the privacy of your home, the *scratch* will be worth it. If you choose to shout, be careful not to make it scary or inappropriate.

might protect our button by pretending someone we admire just walked into the room. Rarely do we lose our self-control when we are trying to impress others. Another option is to imagine we are trying out for a role in a movie. Our child's job is to try and make us angry, but our character is supposed to stay calm at all costs. Our kids are really good at this job, so if necessary be prepared to start the scene over.

Focus on the plan. Having structure or a plan for how we will deal with situations can also help us maintain our self-control. Focusing on what we've already decided to do provides a sense of calm and allows us to be more consistent. This is one of the reasons schools practice fire drills: Having a plan in place increases the odds of people remaining calm and doing what they have been taught to do.

> *FREE Parenting Tip: Self-control comes from within and no one else can do it for us. Even the most controlled person will lose it sometimes. When this happens, ask yourself, "Could I have done worse?" and recognize that you probably could have. If we make it our mission to learn our cues, patterns, and triggers, we will figure it out—perhaps just in time to use our newfound control with our grandchildren.*

Creating Structure

Children need limits. It provides structure and helps to make their world predictable, understandable, and secure. By setting limits for our kids we guide them toward acceptable behaviour, while allowing them room to grow and make mistakes. This helps them become self-confident, resilient human beings.

Why Boundaries are Important

Boundaries are the outside limits—a bottom line that provides a border for what's acceptable versus what is not. If you picture a country, their boundaries (borders), let people know where that country's authority begins and ends. They will make rules and guidelines about who may cross their borders and, what people who are within their boundaries, are allowed to do. You will find huge variations in how strongly these boundaries are enforced and how clearly the borders are defined, but the boundaries themselves will always be there.

Every unit of life has its boundaries; individuals, couples, families, schools, organizations, communities, cities and countries. These boundaries fit with each unit's overriding values and are put in place to support those beliefs. They define the non-negotiable—the bottom line that a person may not cross without serious consequences occurring. A child who disrespects boundaries might find herself expelled from school, clubs, or even her home. A citizen of a country who disrespects boundaries might find himself locked up, exhiled or executed as a result.

It is important for us to become aware of our actual boundaries, so we can be sure we are enforcing what's really important to us. If a teenager striking his mother will result in eviction from the home (family boundary), then a family would be well advised to have rules, guidelines and teaching methods about hitting, self-control and respect for women. If we want our daughter to have a strong sense of herself as an individual (personal boundary), we must model assertiveness, teach her about positive relationships and limit our desire to question her every move.

Our boundaries are part of us, whether we are aware of them or not. Figuring out our bottom line behaviours allows us to be clear about what we are enforcing and why.

Working Within Our Boundaries

> *FREE Parenting Tip: Boundaries and the rules that support them provide limits and structure that help our kids feel safe and cared for. Mutual respect, a sense of belonging, and trust all grow out of clear boundaries.*

Personal boundaries mostly apply to activities that involve our bodies—eating, bathing, touching, sleeping, etc. These boundaries are nonexistent when we are born, since babies rely on others to do everything for them, but slowly build up as the individual gains mastery over her self-care. As she grows, her personal boundaries expand to include a need for privacy and personal decision-making, allowing her to decide the path she will choose in life. By the time she is an adult, these boundaries provide her with an understanding of what she will and will not tolerate from both herself and others.

Personal boundaries for our children, begin with giving our child as much individual control as seems reasonable (given her age, etc.) and fit within the family guidelines we've set out. For example, our family boundary might be about being healthy, so we teach our child she needs to eat vegetables. We honour her personal boundary by letting her choose what kind of vegetable to eat and how much. If instead, we force her to eat something that makes her gag (cooked peas) or to eat everything on her plate, we are telling her not to listen to her body's cues but instead to pay attention only to us. There are two problems with this:

1. We are telling her we know better than her natural guidance system. We cannot know what is going on for her body, so in reality we are misleading her.

2. Personal boundaries and our natural guidance system direct us in making important decisions throughout our lives. If we insist on overriding these systems, what will our child do when we are not there to guide her?

One of the best ways to teach respect for personal boundaries is to model it. Privacy is a boundary that can easily be overlooked in a family environment. Reading diaries, searching drawers, checking through school bags all fall into this category. If we want our kids to clearly understand our off-limit areas (like our purse, wallet, or secret drawer), then we must teach it by respecting their space as well. Many parents question their children (especially teenagers) to help keep them safe, but what they are really doing is crossing the privacy line and sending a message of distrust. Trust and respect for personal space are extremely important boundaries for all of us.

Our family boundaries tend to support our personal limits in a way that everyone in the family can live with. Typically, a family will have only a few boundaries, or bottom-line behaviours, as they encompass main values that rarely change over time. Consider the following examples.

*   Safety is a priority in our family.
*   Healthy living is important to us and is reflected in the majority of our behaviours.
*   In this house, we treat everyone with respect and kindness.

The rules are what we put in place to support these ideas. Often a general rule can be put in place to support the boundary with something more specific created as required. We do not need or want to have rules for every little thing, just a few to support the main idea. Examples of rules supporting a boundary are:

Boundary: Safety is a priority in our family.
General rule: Appropriate safety gear will be worn and used.
Specific rule: Children will wear life jackets when playing
               on the dock.

General rules allow a family space to maneuver while the specific rule clearly spells things out. In this family, a child would know that playing on the dock without a life jacket will result in a consequence (for example, activity removal). This rule doesn't mean he can't negotiate other things, like taking off his life jacket to jump off the dock when an adult is present. The general rule transfers to many situations (biking, rollerblading, and snowboarding), while the specific rule applies only to the water.

Most children will not thank us for our rules and will test them, whine about them, and try to talk us out of them. What they should be clear on, however, is our boundaries and why these principles are in place. With this done, we parents can cling to the knowledge that these boundaries are creating structure for our children that will allow them to go out in the world and thrive.

Family Meetings

Family meetings provide an opportunity for everyone to give input into the functioning of their family home. It is a great forum for sharing expectations, brainstorming household rules, and dealing with discipline issues that apply to everyone.

Outlined below is one way of setting up a family meeting. What's essential is that you have some sort of structure (for example, rules about being open-minded and supportive) so people recognize that it is important. It does not need to be formal, or even regular, but it does need to be taken seriously. Everyone should leave these meetings with an understanding of what was decided and how the decisions made affect them. When people are involved in creating a plan they are more likely to support it.

Some ideas you might include in a family meeting are as follows:

- If meetings will be a common practice in your home, dedicate a regular time for them and do your best to keep to it. Be sure to keep meetings short; half an hour is usually the max for kids twelve and under. Even fifteen minutes is good.

- Have a list posted so anyone can jot ideas down for the next meeting.

- Plan the time; set up a flexible agenda for how the time will look (for example, check-in; concerns, chore schedule, etc., followed by fun activity).

- Take turns at the different roles. Even the young can be in charge of something (planning fun activity, setting up the space, gathering the list).

- Limit complaint time. It seems no matter how positive we try to be, complaining is something that everyone insists on doing at meetings. If so, use creativity to ensure this need is met without allowing it to take over. One idea is to allow each person one minute to voice a complaint. The group then takes two minutes to come up with a resolution. Make a rule that complaints can take up no more than ten percent of the total meeting time. Sometimes just acknowledging the complaints is all that's required.

- Have someone take notes to remind everyone what they agreed upon.

- Do what you agreed to do. If you said you would find more time to play, do that. If your child agreed she would walk the dog nightly and then fails to do so, remind her about what she promised, but be careful not to nag, If she is not doing her task put it back on the list to discuss at the next meeting, or enforce the agreed-upon consequence.

- Take time for fun. Whenever possible set aside time after the meeting to have some fun. Give compliments, play a game, go for a walk together. Make it something your family enjoys, and you'll find they look forward to the next meeting.

Bullying: A Dishonorable Mention

Few things will bring out the *mother bear* in us (even for fathers) like finding out that someone has threatened our cub. I don't mean threats like "You better bring that note by Monday or I'm phoning your mom" (although that can set us off). I mean the type of threat that shakes our child's sense of safety and rocks his secure little world, like "Give me your lunch or you'll be drinking from the toilet." I am talking about threats that come from people who intend harm and have the power (or perceived power) to follow through. I am talking about bullying!

So what can we do to help our child when this happens? First, we need to get our mother bear instinct under control. Yes, we need to help our kids, but we aren't doing any favors by taking over the situation. If we truly want to help them and have a positive impact on their development of self, we have to control our impulse to start roaring and bashing heads in (figuratively, of course) and focus on developing a plan.

The Plan

Step 1: Listen. It's important to understand that any time our kids come to us with a story to share, they are asking us to really hear them. A great way to do this is by using tools like *empathic listening* in which we focus on understanding what the child is feeling, then use that information to connect with him.[17] "It sounds like you're pretty frustrated. I can understand that." The goal is to make sure we hear what our child is saying without reacting and taking over the conversation. Remember, our child is likely afraid and possibly embarrassed because

---

17   Empathic listening is explained further in Chapter 11.

he's afraid. Making it easy for him to talk to us by being a good listener is the least we can do. To do this effectively, we must *avoid* doing certain things, such as the following,

- Making jokes to lighten the mood. "What does the other guy look like?" "She's probably just jealous of your curly hair."

- Defending the bully. "You must have done something for her to treat you so badly"

- Overreacting. "Who does he think he is? Nobody treats my daughter this way and gets away with it!"

Step 2: Give reassurance. The second thing our kids need when they tell us about bullying is to hear that the way they are being treated is not okay. They are in no way deserving of this kind of treatment. "You understand there is nothing wrong with you? It is her and her 'gang' who are the problem here." If your child argues this point, let her vent without your agreeing or disagreeing. If your facial expressions and body language show support and understanding, words are not required. A simple "I see" or "Hmm" can be enough.

Step 3: Encourage inner strength. Our kids need to be told, through both our actions and our words, that while bullying is not okay, they (our kids) are strong enough, smart enough, and resilient enough to handle it. This is critical. If we take over the battle for them, the message they receive is "You're not capable of handling this—I better do it for you." This is a problem because it suggests our child is weak and incapable of dealing with challenging situations. More to the point, what will happen when you're not there to protect them? People who believe problems are too big to handle feel helpless, not resilient.

Step 4: Empower and support. Our goal is to support our child while helping him believe in his own strength and ability. What we do at this point is going to have the greatest impact on our child's sense of ability and self-worth. If we take away his power by trying to fix things for him, we might be doing as much harm as the bully. If instead we empower our child by brainstorming constructive ways to handle the situation, helping him access resources, and, when necessary, advocating on his behalf, he will come out feeling stronger and more capable than when the situation began.[18]

Bullies will come and go throughout our lives and for that they get a dishonorable mention. When these unpleasant situations arise, our children will look to us to figure out how capable or incapable they are to deal with it. If we want our message to strengthen them and let them know they are capable of handling whatever life throws their way, our actions had better back it up.

> *FREE Parenting Tip: Our kids need us to listen to them, give them support, and help them learn skills to protect themselves in bullying situations. Resilient kids are those who are empowered and taught positive ways to stand up for themselves.*

Exercise: Making the Rules

Clarifying our family boundaries and the rules that enforce them is a worthwhile task. Most of us have an idea of what our boundaries are, but we aren't always clear on how we'll enforce them. It is frustrating to have to guess at these boundaries and difficult to follow a rule that

---

18   For further ideas on empowering your children to deal with bullies, check out Izzy Kalman's Web site: http://www.bullies2buddies.com/resources/download-free-manuals

arises only after it's been broken. If you haven't already, it is a good idea to determine what the boundaries, rules, and consequences are in your household and then share them with the people you live with. Depending on the age of your children, this could be completed with everyone involved.

Here are some guidelines for creating the rules. (A worksheet is included following the main points.)

1. Jot down the non-negotiable boundaries that you feel are important for your kids to know about. Keep them simple, positive (for example, *No unhealthy habits* becomes *Healthy living will be reflected in our daily behaviours*) and minimal (three to five should do). Remember, boundaries represent your bottom line behaviours in your family so be sure to choose those that reflect your family values and not just those that society puts out there as important.

2. For each boundary, write out two rules, one general and one specific. For example:

   Boundary #1: *Healthy living will be reflected in our daily behaviours.*

   General rule: *We eat a variety of fruits and vegetables each day.*

   Specific rule: *You must have vegetables with supper.*

3. Choose one of these boundary/rule sets and determine what the consequence will be for not following them. Be sure to use consequences that are relevant, educational, and enforceable. You do not require three consequences for rule-breaking; however, if you are going to do it this way,

the third one should be your most serious consequence. For example:

Rule: *You must have vegetables with supper* consequences:

1st time—*only veggies allowed as snack between supper and bed*

2nd time—*next supper, veggies served and eaten before other food is given*

3rd time—*next supper, veggies only (salad)*

4. Call a family meeting to discuss boundaries, rules, and consequences. If you are parenting with a partner, be sure to compare lists and merge them to make one full set first.

5. Follow-through consistently and calmly when boundaries or rules are tested.

   A great way to deal with rule-breaking is to ask your child to identify the boundary it comes from:

   What do we believe about healthy living?

   Was eating only noodles just now supporting that belief?

   What could you do differently next time to make sure you support it?

   Okay, between now and bed if you want a snack it must be veggies.

6. Notice your kids following the rules and boundaries and provide positive feedback.

   For example: *What a colourful selection of veggies you've chosen today. Great job, I'm sure your body is very happy.*

The rules and boundaries for your family need to fit your values. When children understand why these rules are in place and what makes them important, they are more likely to follow them. Our goal as parents is to teach our kids how to think things through and learn to make good decisions. If they can practice their decision making with the little things (refusing vegetables), by the time they get to the big things in life (drugs, sexual behaviour) they will be more practiced at understanding things like assertiveness, choices and consequences, and be better able to make these potentially life altering decisions.

Establishing Family Boundaries, Rules, and Consequences Worksheet

Boundaries:

_____

_____

_____

_____

_____

Boundary #1: _____

General rule: _____

Specific rule: _____

Consequences:

1st time _____

2nd time _____

3rd time _____

Boundary #2: _____

General rule: _____

Specific rule: _____

Consequences:

1st time _____

2nd time _____

3rd time _____

Boundary #3: _____

General rule: _____

Specific rule: _____

Consequences:

1st time _____

2nd time _____

3rd time _____

Boundary #4: _____

General rule: _____

Specific rule: _____

Consequences:

1st time _____

2nd time _____

3rd time _____

Boundary #5: _____

General rule: _____

Specific rule: _____

Consequences:

1st time _____

2nd time _____

3rd time _____

Part 3

A FREE Parenting Pack

Chapter 8: Packing With Care

My Calling Plan

When my kids were young, I was operating a parent-education business out of my home. Phone calls were a touchy issue since people were often calling for parenting assistance. Having my children act up while I was on the phone would be embarrassing to say the least.

I decided I had to come up with a plan before any big problems could arise. I wrote down a list outlining what I needed from my kids when I was on the phone. I kept it short and created simple rules to follow, complete with rewards and consequences. I explained my strategy to my kids in little pieces (my kids were two and four), and we practiced it with phone calls to friends and family. We developed a secret code for when the phone call was really important and both kids understood that nothing short of an emergency should interrupt those calls.[19]

---

19   My children were taught that anything Mommy was doing could always be interrupted for an emergency. Thankfully, we haven't had very many.

When possible, I'd plan my phone calls to happen during our afternoon quiet time when the kids were typically napping, drawing, looking at books, or colouring. When the phone would ring or before I'd dial, I'd announce what I was doing and start the call. If they got too loud (playing) or tried talking to me during the call, I'd give the prearranged signal that I shouldn't be interrupted. If they ignored the signal, I would ask to ring the caller back and hang up. My kids then went to their bedrooms where they would stay until I had phoned the person back and finished my call. There was no discussion or negotiating once I hung up—the damage had been done and the consequences were calmly enforced.

If they quieted down after the signal (or never required the signal), I would finish my phone call and we'd celebrate our success. Our rewards were things like playing outside, eating a Popsicle, watching a favorite show, or playing a game of their choice.

When the phone calls weren't prearranged, it was a bit tougher but still worked. If we were in the middle of some high-energy game when the phone rang, I either let the machine get it or would ask if I could return the call. If I needed to take the call, I'd signal to the kids and make it up to them afterward.

On other occasions, my kids would be playing nicely when I answered the phone but a few minutes into the conversation would start acting up. When this happened, I'd give them the signal or, if necessary, ask my caller to wait while I let them know I was on the phone. If my kids cooperated, I'd finish my call. If they didn't, the rest of the plan went into place.

This didn't work all the time, and my kids definitely tested the plan. I found that because I had a plan and had been clear about it with my kids, it was easier to stay calm and put consequences in place when things went awry. Although I thought I might be embarrassed to have to interrupt my phone call to deal with my kids, the callers seemed to understand and were often thrilled with my process. I also became aware of the amount of time I was spending on the phone and made a conscious effort to decrease my daytime calls.

Overall, my kids became pretty respectful when I was on the phone, and I experienced very few annoying or embarrassing phone situations as a result.

Some other telephone tips I've heard over the years include the following.

- Have a basket of toys that come out only during phone calls.

- Have a grab bag with little (dollar-store) items the kids can "grab" from.

- Have a special snack bag with treats the kids get to eat only when their caregiver is on the phone.

- Take a moment during a lengthy phone call to stop and praise the kids for good behaviour. "I really like the way the two of you are playing so nicely while I'm on the phone—keep up the great work!"

- Create a chart that the kids put a sticker on every time they successfully allow you to have an uninterrupted phone call, which eventually results in a reward.

Our Hidden Baggage

When it comes to parenting, we carry a lot of baggage with us. This pack of information is made up of techniques and strategies that were used on us in our youth, whether they worked or not, whether we liked them or not. In other words, if a teacher made us stand in a corner with gum stuck to the end of our nose, the idea of *humiliation* will be something we carry. If we really didn't like how this strategy felt, we might believe we would never use it and not even know we are carrying it at all.

Interestingly though, it is there and sometimes will resurface in ways we never imagined. For example, you might warn your child not to choose grape drink to bring in the car because if it spills (again) it will make a mess of his clothes. It spills and now there is a purple stain down the front of his yellow shirt and beige pants. Frustrated that he didn't listen to your wisdom, you make a big deal out of how awful it looks, telling him he should be embarrassed of his stained clothes. You then take him along to all the stops you had initially planned making jokes with other adults about his purple shirt. Sound a bit like humiliation?

The important piece to understand is that this idea, right or wrong, is in your parenting pack. The teacher might or might not have done it to be mean. You might or might not use it to be mean. The fact remains that, in both cases, humiliation was used to try to force a child to think about what he has done, recognize his error, and behave better the next time. It is something you know and therefore bring along with you.

This explains why we will catch ourselves doing things that we swore we would never do. Or how we can open our mouth and hear our mother's words come tumbling out. These actions can create a feeling of guilt and sense of failure if we aren't aware that they are with us. Those strategies that were used on us often, or that were accompanied by intense emotion, will always be around.

When we need a parenting tool, we reach into our pack and pull one out. When we are stressed, angry, or otherwise bothered, we tend to reach for tactics that have an element of hurt or punishment to them— not because we are bad people, but because we are looking for a strategy that fits how we feel. When this happens, and the child doesn't seem to care about the consequences, we will reach for something harsher.

The challenge becomes learning new ideas and practicing with them so we can replace some *undesirable* punishments with ideas that fit our parenting philosophy. Like any new plan, the tendency will be to go back to the familiar. If we resist that urge and make ourselves use our new skills, over time we will become more comfortable with new strategies and less likely to use the ineffective old one.

So, if you find yourself standing over your child, waving your finger, and telling her she is very, very bad, know that your mother (or teacher or coach) has not just teleported in and taken over your body. Instead, you have grabbed a tactic from your parenting pack that someone else has given to you. You still need to take responsibility for your actions, but at least this can help you understand your response and perhaps be a bit more forgiving.

> *FREE Parenting Tip: Our parenting pack is made up of strategies and tactics used by other people to get our attention when we were younger. We carry this pack wherever we go, so it's a good idea to know what's inside.*

Unloading the Heavy Stuff

Most of us have strategies in our parenting pack that we would prefer not to use. While we might respect the way our parents (and other adults) raised us, lots of older tools do not fit with what we see as acceptable today or do not meet our parenting goals. Punishments like spanking, the strap, arm grabbing/twisting, threatening, excessive privilege removal, or consequences (scrubbing the toilet with a toothbrush), are all tools we recognize might not be the best way to teach right from wrong.

These strategies gain compliance by creating fear in the child—fear of pain, loss, embarrassment, or of the person threatening the act. Most of us can understand that compliance through fear is not effective, as it tends to damage self-esteem, sends conflicting messages (for example, I'm hurting you because I love you and don't want you to get hurt) and has the potential to escalate into something dangerous.

For many of us, these techniques don't work because we are not raising our children to fear us. As a result, when we pull out a fear-based tool, our children have nothing to link the underlying threat to. It's like the family dog growling at us when she's never bitten before. We might be surprised by her growl, but chances are we won't take her threat seriously.

Another problem with these tactics is that they are often pulled out when we are angry, stressed, embarrassed, or at our wits' end. Our child ignores us, our self-control snaps, and next thing we know we've "bitten" our child! The guilt, embarrassment, and regret are often too much to take.

These tools are usually in our pack because other people used them on us. We do not have to use them, but unless we are aware of them and why they are not effective, we are very likely to pull them out. If we allow this to happen, we will desensitize to this parenting style and begin to justify their use. Over time, we will start to see fear-based tools as the only strategies that really get our child's attention.

These strategies can appear to be effective because they often result in the child stopping what she was doing and changing her behaviour to do as we asked. But this is only part of the equation. The real test of whether or not the tool worked would be for the child to have learned what she did wrong, why it's not okay, and what she might do the next time this situation arises. Instead, she's likely learning one or more of the following lessons.

- People who are bigger can hurt people who are smaller (bullying).

- When you do something wrong, be sure not to get caught (sneakiness).

- Making mistakes is wrong and you should fear it (perfectionism).

- My parent is mean and I hate him/her (resentment/revenge).

- People who love you will hurt you (helplessness/abuse justification).

Parents using these strategies are not usually mean people; they are simply doing the best they can with what they know.

There are two arguments I hear from parents to justify the use of these tools. The first is that *as long as these tools are not used in anger* they are a good way to get their child's attention. Even without arguing about the effectiveness of the tool itself, there is still something else to consider.

When we are not angry, we are more apt to use our creativity to try to figure out another way of gaining our child's compliance. Parents who are most likely to pull out these fear tools are already at their wits' end, stressed, or otherwise pushed. Rarely will a parent today use these outdated methods when they are feeling calm and in control. In other words most parents use these strategies *only* when they are angry.

The second argument I hear is *my parents used it on me, and I turned out okay.* Our world has changed from when we were growing up. We are constantly learning and evolving. Yes, we want our kids to respect us. But fear us? Once we know, and understand why these strategies are ineffective, how can we, in good conscience, continue to use them?

Replacing Our Heavy Tools

Recognizing that these techniques are not helping us be the kind of parent we would like to be, the question becomes *What can we do about it?* The first step has already been accomplished. Awareness is the key to making changes to what's in our parenting pack. In fact, just becoming aware of how we talk to our children (tone of voice, words, and body language) can make a huge difference in our relationship with our child.

The second step is a bit more intensive because of the volume of work that is required. Fear-based tools are very powerful. There are plenty of other effective strategies, but none that, on its own, easily replaces a fear-based one.

For example, time-out is the tool most people are familiar with as an alternative to spanking. Time-out, when used properly, can be a useful way to help kids learn self-control. It does not, however, satisfy the strong emotions that are often surging through us just before we spank. The only way a time-out can help in a situation like that is when the parent is the one who takes it.

This means fear-based strategies can only become a thing of the past if we replace them with a variety of other tools. Ideas like time-out, choices, logical consequences, privilege-removal, or problem solving can be used effectively depending on the situation. There are no tools that are going to work perfectly in every situation or with every child and often prevention will be a much better way to deal with things. It is up to us to fill our parenting pack with a variety of strategies that allow us to choose the best tool for the job and then do our best to control our response enough to make the best choice.

> *FREE Parenting Tip: Becoming aware of the outdated gear we are carrying in our parenting pack can help us lighten our load. If we look carefully at what we are trying to achieve when we correct our kids and learn tools that deliver that message, we will get better results and build a stronger relationship with our child.*

136

Knowing How to Pack

One of the most challenging aspects of parenting is feeling confident we are *doing the right thing* when our kids make a mistake. If there is something I've learned about raising kids, it's that there is no right or wrong way for doing anything. The kindest of words can be turned into a cruel manipulation technique with a simple tone of voice, and tools that on the surface appear hurtful can be done (albeit rarely) in a way that provides effective learning.[20]

This means we shouldn't immediately write off the strategies we like to use in support of those currently being promoted as best. There have definitely been instances where *best practices* have turned out to be far less than "best" and have caused more grief than benefits. People who adopt these tools despite concerns about effectiveness eventually drop them and then feel resistance to trying new tools in the future.

I believe we should give serious thought to our overall goals with our children and decide whether or not our current strategies are working toward that end. If they are, then we can continue using them. If they aren't, small adaptations might be needed or, on occasion, new ideas might be in order. Adopting new things just because someone else tells us we must, damages self-confidence and makes us second-guess our usual ability.

---

20 While I'm not an advocate of hitting children, some parents talk about the respectful way they were spanked and the learning they took from it. Others share stories of fathers engaging in a fist fight with their teenage boys that taught far more than it hurt. These methods seem counterproductive to me, yet I'm open-minded enough to recognize that, in these cases, they might have been carried out respectfully.

Kids listen better and pay more attention to what we ask, if we are predictable and consistent with our messages and follow-through. They also pay more attention if we choose our battles carefully, resist nagging, avoid overcorrecting, and are careful not to overuse the word no.

Making good use of the natural tools we have, like our voices and our relationship with our children, will also work to our advantage. This means instead of calling a request to our child from a different room, we walk over to him, put our hand lightly on his shoulder, and talk to him. This eliminates the question of whether or not he heard us and lets him know that we mean business. The Triple P, Positive Parenting Program from Australia suggests we then give him time (about ten seconds) to process our request and do as we asked. After a silent count to ten, if he doesn't move we can calmly repeat our request. If he chooses not to listen after a second pause, consequences can be put in place.

Any request that requires our children to shift gears (stop what they are doing and start something else) will work better if we give them a few minutes warning ahead of time. Although our schedule might be clear to us, it's not apparent to others, especially our children. When we let our kids know in advance to prepare for a change, they are much more likely to comply. A ten-minute warning before bed or a five-minute warning before leaving a party will always be helpful. If my kids politely questioned the time provided, I'd ask them how much time they needed and then negotiate from there. Often, I would suggest ten minutes and they would make a counteroffer of seven!

Another idea to keep our kids working with us is to prepare for outings in advance.[21] This means rather than throwing a few items in

---

[21]   **Sanders, Matthew,** *Triple P Select Practitioner Training* **(University of Queensland, 2004).**

our bag and heading out to the store, bank, or doctor's office, we take the time to think about what the challenges might be for us and our kids. We decide ahead of time what we can do to prevent challenges (a toy for bored kids, snack for hunger) and develop consequences or rewards for these behaviours. We let our kids know in simple, age-appropriate terms what will be expected of them and how we will celebrate when everything works out (a stop at the park for a swing; two extra stories at bedtime, etc). Establishing a warning signal for problem behaviour is also a good idea, so our kids can have an opportunity to use their self-control and change what they are doing. The warning should only be used as planned (for example, said once calmly) and then the consequences come into play.

If things go bad during our outing, it's easier to stay calm and use consequences we've already prepared. If things go well, our simple celebration reinforces our success. This doesn't mean we can never do anything spontaneously, it just means the more we prepare in advance, the greater the chances that our experience will be positive.

There are some things that will make all of our parenting strategies more effective, such as the following:

- Clear expectations (clarity of what behaviour is acceptable versus unacceptable) with an understanding that people won't always measure up to them.

- An understanding that mistakes are an opportunity to learn, not a sign of weakness. Discipline should allow a child to take responsibility for her behaviour without making her feel faulty as a person.

- Recognition that life is gray while most tools are black and white. Be willing to adapt tools to fit the situation and the people involved.

- Communication that builds relationships and models respect.

- Calm, controlled, and consistent follow-through.

Clarity, creativity, respect, and planning are necessary parts to whatever strategies we decide to include in our parenting pack. Preventing problems by thinking them through in advance and ensuring our message is clear and unmistakable can reap us many great rewards.

> *FREE Parenting Tip: The difference between a good or bad parenting tool is often how we are using it. Having a variety of tools in our parenting pack, planning things out in advance, and being clear with our requests makes it easier for us to use our tools well.*

Strategies That Build

Human beings are social creatures who are strongly influenced by their relationships with others. When it comes to guiding our kids toward acceptable behaviours, we have much greater influence when they like us as people. As a result, it is worth it to focus on building a connection with our kids for more than just the obvious reasons.

Four powerful building tools that when used regularly can have a huge influence on the quality of our relationships are outlined below. The more these building strategies are put into practice in our lives the greater the amount of respect in our relationships. The greater the amount of respect in our relationships the more our family will want to work with us instead of against us.

Spending Time with Our Children

The first, and perhaps most obvious, way to build connection with our kids is to spend time with them. Recognizing that many of our days come with a long "to do" list and not a lot of time, I'm not talking about dedicating huge amounts of time to playing or chatting together, although obviously this would be helpful to forming connection.[22] Instead, I'm talking about looking for little opportunities to acknowledge what our kids are doing, show interest in a positive way, share affection, and then continue on with our tasks.

When kids are little, parents will often sneak past their happily playing child to finish the laundry or whatever else they have to get done. Their concern is the child will never let them go if discovered and there is so much to do. While this might be true sometimes, most kids are better able to deal with our needs when we take a moment to connect with them and then are upfront about what we must do next. For example, "Wow, look at the town you've set up with your cars. It looks like a fun place to drive. What's this over here?" After a minute or two, "Okay, I have to go and start supper. I'll come back in a bit to see what else you've done."

If our child fusses and asks us to stay, we can be friendly yet firm. "I enjoy watching you play and would love to stay longer. Right now I have to make supper. I'll come back and check on you soon." The more we practice these kinds of interactions, the more our kids see that we are interested and available yet still have tasks of our own.

---

22   See Chapter 4's *Building Relationships Chart* **for other simple ways to build connection.**

As our kids mature, these moments might change to a quick shoulder massage while doing homework, a short conversation about the day, or an acknowledgment about something new we've noticed, "Is that a new song you're singing/game you're playing/shoes you're wearing, I don't recognize it."

Using Deliberate and Effective Feedback

Another strategy that builds both our relationship and our child's sense of self-worth is to clearly tell them when they have done something that we like. Using effective feedback builds self-esteem and provides information they can file away for future use. This is less about praise like "Good job" or "Way to go!" and more about describing what they did that we liked. For example; "I love the way you two played so quietly while I was napping. That was very considerate." Another example might be "Thanks for feeding the cat. It makes my morning easier when you help with the chores."

It feels good to have our efforts noticed and it's helpful to know exactly what we did that is being noticed. Once our child is aware of a certain positive behaviour, a simple wink, note, or hug, might be all that's required to show we notice and appreciate what he has done (for example, winking at him when if he feeds the cat for the third day in a row).

Recognizing Our Mistakes and Apologizing When We Are Wrong

We build respect and connection in a relationship if we are able to recognize when we are in the wrong and take full responsibility for it. This means if we lose our control, overreact, break a promise, forget something important, or make a mistake, we acknowledge what we have done and apologize for our behaviour.

Many people have been taught that apologies from an adult to a child are at best unnecessary and at worst undesirable. This is interesting, since a forced apology seems to be the most common tool in every adult's parenting pack. "You tell Timmy you are sorry you hurt his feelings, right now!"

When we apologize to our children, we benefit in many ways. First, our relationship strengthens as our child recognizes we are taking responsibility for our actions and are truly sorry. Respect and trust grow out of this. Second, we are role-modeling a behaviour we want our kids to learn. Third, an apology from a parent reinforces the idea that, while it might not always seem true, parents are in fact human and do make mistakes. In our children's eyes, this is important information for them to understand; we do not know everything and we are willing to admit it.

Finally, our apology provides us with an opportunity to model what a good apology looks like. It contains no buts, excuses, or minimizing of our behaviour, just an apology.

- I'm sorry, I was wrong.

- I'm sorry. I should never have yelled at you that way.

- I'm so sorry. I hope you will let me make this up to you.

Recognize that an apology does not include demanding forgiveness. All we can give is the apology and hope that, in time, the other person will choose to forgive us. Thankfully, kids seem to recognize the personal benefits of forgiveness and tend to forgive quite easily.

Giving Our Kids the Benefit of the Doubt

> *FREE Parenting Tip: The relationships we build in our families determine how effective our parenting strategies will be. We can begin building strong family foundations by spending time together, providing effective feedback, apologizing when we are wrong, and giving our kids the benefit of the doubt.*

Instead of judging our children's actions and getting angry, we do better to become investigators and try to understand why our child acted the way she did.

Everything that happens around us is filtered through our own system before it is given meaning. When we see, hear, smell, taste, or touch something, we use the data available and how it makes us feel to decide how to react. The problem is we are reacting based on our understanding of the situation and not on reality. If instead, we could really try to understand the other person's point of view, we have a much greater chance of getting a clear picture. This helps us avoid misunderstandings, builds respect, and teaches patience. People always have a reason for what they have done and, at the moment of choosing, that reason seemed like a good one.

Try to make it a habit to give your child the benefit of the doubt and try to figure out why she did what she did. Put on your investigator's hat and provide her with an opportunity to explain. This does not mean demanding "Why did you do that!" but calmly asking, "Can you help me to understand why you were kicking the cat?" or "What did you mean when you said you are running away forever?"

Remember, a good investigator keeps an open mind and does not allow emotions to interfere with the facts. Curiosity is the only emotion you need to do this.

Using building tools such as these helps create an environment in which families want to work together. If we were building a house, we'd spend a fair amount of time ensuring our foundation was sturdy and long-lasting. Let's make sure our family foundation holds up for generations to come.

FREE Tool Analysis

The strategies we use with our children can be divided into two broad categories. The first group is the building tools, which are meant to create a strong, mutually respectful relationship so that our kids want to work with us and be part of our team. The second is the fixing tools geared toward changing behaviours or helping our child fix a mistake she has made.

There are many strategies available to us, some that are extremely effective and others that really are not. To assist with recognizing a good fixing tool I like to use the acronym FREE. If the strategy we are using is *F*unctional, *R*espectful, *E*ffective, and *E*asy, I'm definitely going to keep it around.

Functional: The tool we are using should teach our child something relevant to his error. If our tool does not allow us to link the consequence to the mistake, learning will be minimal. A good link example might be that when the child rides his bike without a helmet, his bike is put away for two days.

Respectful: If we want our kids to be respectful to others (and us) we must be sure to model this behaviour. If our tool attacks our child personally, it will cause resentment or lowered self-esteem. When we deal with the mistake instead of his character, he learns more. Telling him in a matter-of-fact voice that his bike is going away will do more than reminding him he is always forgetting things.

Effective: Discipline is done to modify our children's behaviour. Our best fixing strategies should result in *improved* behaviour from our kids. For example, our child wears his bike helmet without a fuss as a result of two days without his bike.

Easy: Parenting is tough enough without our discipline tools adding extra work. If a strategy is too difficult for us to be consistent and follow through with, then it's hurting more than helping. Disciplining our kids should be more work for them than for us. Our main job is to provide consistent follow-through, so make sure the tool is easy for you to enforce. In the bike example, our only job is to ensure the bike is put away for two days. If necessary, a simple lock can do that job.

Exercise: What Are You Packing?

This exercise will help you think about what's in your parenting pack by guiding you through a process of past and present self-analysis.

For Part I, open your memories up to parents, teachers, club leaders, coaches, neighbors … in fact any adult who had a hand in telling you what to do as a child.

Part I: Taking Inventory

1. On a piece of paper, draw your parenting pack. (Just a rectangle will work fine.)

2. Pretend you have been nominated for the Parent of the Year award and will be provided with one minute to give a thank-you speech when you receive the trophy. Above your pack, write who you would thank for helping you reach the level of knowledge and skill that you currently have as a parent (for example, parents, second-grade teacher, authors, religious leaders, hockey coach).

   These are the people who inspire you to grow and expand.

3. Think about those people who, when you were young, treated you in a way that you really didn't like—specifically in regard to discipline/punishment. You don't need to write names, but instead think about the specific strategies or tools they used to try to make you comply with their wishes (for example, yelling, ear-pinching, kneeling in a corner, reverse psychology, threats). Write them in the body of the pack.

   These are the tools that you wish you didn't use but will find yourself using (or thinking about using) when you are stressed.

4. Reflect on the strategies you have learned or further developed as an adult. Write them in the body of the pack as well. If there are tools you know about and would like to use, but currently

do not, write them in the main pack too and circle them (for example, patience, empathy, logical consequences, effective voice, listening).

These are the tools you want to practice and gain comfort with using.

5. Finally, think about the kinds of skills you believe children are going to need in order to be successful in the world. Your parenting pack is used to teach social and emotional skills, so be sure to focus on those areas for this list. Write these ideas along the bottom of the paper, outside of the box (for example, communication skills, assertiveness, cooperation, self-control, independence).

These are the tools you are hoping your children will have by the time they are adults.

Part II: Analyzing Your Gear

Now that we have an idea of what is in your pack, let's take a look at any tools we might want to study more thoroughly, as well as any that might need adaptations or replacement.

1. Mark any strategies in your pack that are fear-based. If you are unsure what is fear-based, try to imagine your child taller and stronger than you are. Could you still use this strategy and gain compliance? Is there a threatening tone to your voice when you use this tool? What is it about the tool that makes your child listen?

2. Using a different colour (or mark), note any tools you use numerous times a day or week. Anything done over and over

becomes monotonous, for both the giver and the receiver. If you always use time-out when your kids misbehave, it will become repetitive and your kids will tune out the learning benefits.

3. Put a check mark beside any strategies that guide your child toward appropriate behaviour and help him grow stronger in the process. Put an X beside any that focus on the child personally rather than his behaviour and make him feel bad about himself as a person (for example, "Bad boy, why don't you ever listen?").

4. Mark as your ultimate tools the strategies you pull out when you must have your way and your child is not working with you. These are your power cards and should be used only when compliance is absolutely required. If you are using them to get your way at other times, understand that you are weakening both them and your Parent Power.

Part III: Parenting Style Questions

Sometimes our tools are fine, but our parenting style will be making them ineffective. Becoming aware of how our habits influence our parenting strategies can make it a lot easier to understand why things aren't working and exactly where changes are required.

• Do you repeat yourself many times to your children before you follow-through? When this happens, you are falling into a parenting pit that can cause you much grief. When kids learn incessant whining gets them what they want, they become incessant whiners. When kids figure out you mean business only when your voice hits a certain octave, they will come to respond to only that note.

- Are you spending a lot of time explaining things to your child? If so, does your child get a glazed look in her eyes as soon as you start talking and only pretend to listen? Mini-lectures (and especially lengthy ones) are never fun to listen to and, given a choice, most of us will tune them out. When parents do a lot of talking, kids stop listening.

- Is your behaviour contradicting what you are telling your child to do? When we tell our kids to stop something, yet laugh or smile when they continue, we are sending a very mixed message. Making people laugh feels good, and the message to stop will seem insignificant compared to that good feeling. Be sure your energy matches your request. If you say stop—mean it!

- Are you modeling the strategies you really want your child to learn? Tools like assertiveness, patience, determination, compromising, synergizing, negotiating, and conflict resolution will be internalized more by watching and practicing.

Analyzing our parenting pack helps us to see what areas we need to work on as well as those things we are already doing well. Since your pack is something you carry with you daily, you might as well make sure you are packing the tools you really want to take along.

Chapter 9: Making Common Strategies FREE

My Power Play

When my daughter was young and we were going somewhere she didn't want to go, she would simply refuse to go. This was a problem when someone in the family needed to be somewhere by a certain time. She was too young to leave at home alone and totally determined not to give in.

Through trial and error I figured out that privilege-removal got her attention better than any other tool I had tried (and I tried a lot of tools). In this case, I explained to her that sometimes parents simply need their children to cooperate. If she wouldn't and it was causing a problem for the rest of the family, I would use my Parent Power to make it happen. This meant I could and would start removing privileges as soon as she dug in her heels and would continue to do so until she complied. Typically, I would start with whatever was her favorite item at the moment (television, movies, computer, or gaming system) and remove it one day at a time. When I reached one week gone for an item, I would switch to the next:

"You need to come with us and we need to leave now. You have ten seconds before I start using my Parent Power." After ten seconds: "There goes the computer for tomorrow (Tuesday)." After five more seconds: "Wednesday." After five more: "Thursday." Finally: "Okay that's one week of computer, now we're moving on to T.V."

The first time she lost all four items for two weeks (I admit I was starting to panic) before she angrily cooperated. She managed to take a week off that sentence for good behaviour and, after that, had only one other testing situation before requiring a simple reminder to gain compliance. In other words, this process quickly taught her that sometimes you have to do things for other people just because, and, while you don't have to enjoy it, you do need to comply.

My main job was to stay calm, be respectful, be consistent, and follow-through with what was removed. When she would ask to use the computer before the end of the removal period, I would respond with something like, "I wish you could. Two more days and you'll have it back, thanks to your good behaviour." If she started to argue, whine, or otherwise act up, I would ignore her (usually by pretending to read), and she would lose her good behaviour advantage for that day.

An interesting aside to this, these removals worked despite the fact that in a normal week she got only one hour per weekday (two for weekends) to spend on all four of those things combined. It was losing the right to that privilege that made it work, not the amount of time she was losing. I'm happy to say those days are long gone, which is interesting because now she is old enough to be left at home alone.

For Every Action ...

When our children break a rule, make a mistake, or misbehave, we want them to learn from what they have done. We know that for every action there is a reaction and for every effect there was a cause. It is important our kids learn this idea as well.

This is not about punishing a child to teach him a lesson or make him pay for what he has done. It is more about helping him become aware of the natural fallout from his behaviour. It is meant to instill self-discipline and teach the child to do what is right in the future whether someone is there to enforce it or not.

Often nature will deal out consequences for us, and we don't have to intervene for our kids to learn a lesson. For example, if a child decides not to bring her jacket and it is a cool evening, the natural consequence will be for her to be cold. If we really want this learning to take place, we do not have to do anything and the cool discomfort our child feels will provide some learning. It might not be enough to teach her to always bring a jacket in the future, but it is providing a better learning experience than any we could supply.

Where this falls apart is when we interfere with nature. Perhaps we feel Mother Nature is too cruel and we give the child our jacket, extra sweater, or blanket so she doesn't need to suffer. Knowing she still needs to learn a lesson for choosing not to bring her coat, we try to straighten her out verbally: "Next time you bring your jacket like mommy told you, right!?" These words send a mixed message: If you want to be warm next time you must look after yourself, but in case you forget I will do it for you.

In many cases, nature will do a much better job of teaching little livable lessons than we will. Debating how cold it needs to be to warrant intervention is not an issue here, since if it was very cold with the risk of frostbite or hypothermia, you wouldn't have given her a choice to bring a jacket in the first place. This is about allowing nature to provide consequences when it is possible and safe to do so without rescuing and losing the effective learning.

The following are examples of natural consequences:

- Going to bed hungry after choosing not to eat supper

- Being too warm or cold after choosing not to dress properly

- Losing a toy after not checking under the hotel bed before leaving

- Being bored after choosing not to bring activities

- Being tired after staying up too late at a sleepover

- Being thirsty after choosing not to bring water

Of course, there are times when nature would deal out consequences but we are not willing (or able) to let this happen. For example, letting a child run across the road could naturally mean his getting hit by a car. Since this is an example we can't let happen, we have to figure out a different way to teach our kids. We do this by creating the consequence ourselves.

These are called logical consequences and as such are meant to be logically thought out and enforced. If they are determined in advance, they are easier for us to put into place and have a greater chance of teaching our child something useful. To use logical consequences successfully, we must ensure they are well thought out and calmly delivered.

The following are examples of logical consequences:

- Child ignores safety line and plays too close to the road; child comes inside for designated amount of time (five minutes, half an hour)

- Child refuses to wear sunscreen or protective clothing; child is allowed to play only in shaded area or stay inside

- Child leaves DVDs all over the floor after going through them; child is not allowed to watch DVDs for a day

- Child points a toy gun at a person; gun is taken away for a specified period

- Youth spends evening on the phone/computer instead of doing homework; computer/phone is off limits until homework is done (for a day or a week)

- Teen comes home after curfew without calling; teen is required to be home half an hour earlier next time for every five minutes he was late this time

I taught my kids that if their behaviour needed correcting, I would give them a prearranged warning so they would know their behaviour was not okay and have an opportunity to change it. If they heeded the warning and changed their behaviour, all was forgiven. If they ignored the warning, the consequence was put into place with no further discussion.

> *FREE Parenting Tip: Natural and logical consequences help our children learn right from wrong. To use them effectively we must be able to stay calm, be creative, and allow Mother Nature to take her course.*

Sometimes, when my kids were younger, I would ask them to help me come up with consequences for troublesome behaviours they were habitually doing. I would explain why I felt those behaviours were not okay and tell them it would be a good idea for us to come up with a consequence to help them break this habit.

For example, when my son was a preschooler, he loved to jump on the couch. I was somewhat concerned that the couch springs couldn't take that kind of regular abuse and asked him to help me come up with a consequence. Because he was not yet good at the alphabet and had been trying to learn it, we agreed that he would recite the alphabet every time he forgot and jumped on the couch.

Although the couch-jumping did not stop immediately, it did decrease drastically and my son learned the alphabet. He did not feel like he was being punished, which was important because I did not feel couch-jumping required a major correction. If I had felt couch-jumping was a safety issue (if it was a high couch or had a coffee table in front), there would have been an immediate corrective strategy put in place.

As a parenting tool, consequences work well if we allow ourselves to be creative and focus on the learning that is taking place. It teaches our children predictability, responsibility, self-discipline, and the idea that for every action there is a reaction. It helps us practice creativity, consistency, and self-control. With Mother Nature there is no settling of scores attached to a consequence, just an end result. If we can remember to use nature as our role model for creation and delivery of consequences, it is a tool worth having in our parenting pack.

Key points to remember when using consequences are the following:

- When possible allow nature to decide the consequence without your interference.

- Be consistent, calm, and quick to put preplanned logical consequences into place.

- Be sure the consequence fits the crime as closely as possible.

- It is the *certainty,* not the severity, that makes a consequence effective. Mother Nature does not drop the temperature thirty degrees more because a child refused to bring a jacket. This is about learning, not about "teaching a lesson."

- If your child does not seem upset by the consequence, that is okay. This process is not punishment but rather about guiding your child toward appropriate behaviour. A person who makes a mistake and then cheerfully fixes it should be applauded.

- It is okay to tell your child you will need time to come up with a consequence for an unexpected behaviour that requires correction. Consequences should not be given out when you are angry. If your child is pushing your buttons, take time to regain your self-control before acting.

- Avoid threatening your child with a consequence when you already have one in place. For example, if your child has been told she'll have to go inside if she goes past the garden,

- take her inside as soon as she crosses that line. Telling her that she must come back or she'll have to go inside is putting the consequence out as a threat and weakening it at the same time.

- Whenever possible, provide your child with an opportunity to try again later. If you've taken away a toy gun because your son pointed it at his baby sister, give it back to him after the allotted time (for example, five minutes) and remind him of the rules of use. If he does it again, take the gun away for a much longer period (for example, a day).

- When possible, provide planned warnings to give your kids a chance to practice self-control.[23]

Stop, or That Privilege Is Gone

Privilege removal is a tool that most parents use in one form or another. It is similar to logical consequences in that we are removing something as a result of our child's misbehaviour. The name stems from the idea that our children's freedom, along with the items they have and their permission to use those items, are all privileges that can be lost to bad behaviour. A lot of the key points for consequences are relevant to

---

23   Thomas Phelan's *1-2-3 Magic* **provides a nice structure for using warnings effectively.**

privilege-removal, although if we want to get the most out of this tool there are some important differences to keep in mind.

For example, if our child gets in trouble for texting on his cell phone at school, his phone might be removed as a consequence, whether we gave it to him or not. The phone was part of the misbehaviour (a natural link) and has been taken as a result.

If, on the other hand, our child is skipping classes, we might take away the privilege of using his cell phone to get his attention and let him know this behaviour is not desirable. To make this tool effective, we must make the link to the misbehaviour obvious. For example: "Son, we got you a cell phone because we felt you were reliable and working hard to do well in life. Skipping classes at school to 'hang' with your friends does not fit with those qualities. We're taking your cell phone away for a week while you think about those virtues and how you can bring them back into your world. We'll look forward to hearing what you come up with."[24]

An important note to this is we cannot remove a privilege we have not given our child in the first place. Imagine a neighbor telling you that because you woke him up by cutting the lawn early in the morning, he is taking away your lawn mower. It sounds ludicrous, and it is; if he didn't give it, he can't take it away.

---

24 Sometimes, with privilege-removal, you can leave the removal time open to *being convinced*, "When you can convince us you're ready to practice these qualities again, you may have your cell phone back." If you are impossible to convince or tend to feel guilty and give in, this alternative will not work well for you.

Similarly, if our child earns a school trip by working hard and doing well at school and we take it away for misbehaviour at home, any learning will be in the form of resentment.

In this case, we are targeting the cell phone because we know it is something he will miss. It could just have easily been his music, television time, or permission to go to a party. If our son has purchased the cell phone himself, we would be better off to target something we did buy and he uses regularly, like his guitar.

Since privilege-removal involves removing the *right* to do something—like watch television, listen to music, chat on the Internet, drive the car, etc.—there is often no obvious link between what the child has done wrong and the privilege she is losing as a result. This means we must create a link if we want positive learning to occur. If we cannot come up with any link to the misbehaviour, then removing that privilege is not going to help us reach our parenting goals. Without a link, many kids will have nothing to focus on but bitterness or revenge. With a bit of creativity, there is usually a link that can be established even if you have to dig deep to find it.

We also need to recognize that this strategy is not great for a parent who is not home to enforce what has been taken away. If you work late and your child is home on his own, it would be very hard to ensure he is not using the T.V. In this case it is probably better to choose a tool you can enforce a bit easier.

Privilege-removal can be a useful tool providing we don't overdo it. If we take away too much too fast, our kids get caught up in the injustice of it and the learning element is lost. If we take things away for too long and then give them back before the allotted time is up, we teach our children to keep at us because we might just give in. Few of us enjoy having our privileges taken away. When we use this tool respectfully, we help our kids learn how to think and how to take responsibility for their behaviour. A lot of lessons in life are learned by losing privileges, so our kids might as well make that connection as early as possible.

> *FREE Parenting Tip: Privilege-removal can be a great way to get our kids' attention, although to be effective it requires a link to the misbehaviour and some thought about the items we are taking. Use it carefully.*

You Are So Grounded

Grounding is a tool that many people use with their kids because it was used on them. The main idea is to restrict the child's freedom, forcing her to stay home (or in her bedroom) at a time in her life when she is normally very social. Typically, it is tied with privilege-removal, meaning that not only will the child's freedom be limited but also the things she is allowed to do.

There are a few challenges with this tool, including the following:

1. Grounding creates a lot of work for the adult in charge. For grounding to be effective, someone has to enforce the penalty and keep tabs on the offender. This can mean anything from listening for the bedroom door or telephone calls, to watching out for nighttime window escapes.

2. This tool can give the punished child a lot of power over family outings. For example, if a plan had been made for the family to go out to dinner (perhaps to celebrate an important event), a grounding creates a dilemma. The child has been grounded until

the following weekend. To take her with you would contradict the grounding lesson, but leaving her at home alone would mean unrestricted freedom. Cancelling your dinner would give her too much power, and granting a one-night pass defeats the purpose.

3. Often there is no link between the grounding and what the child has done. This limits the learning and tends to shift the child's focus from what she did wrong (*it's not okay to steal*) to the injustice of it all.

4. A problem arises when the child being grounded is not very social. The parent knows taking away her freedom is not going to teach much of a lesson but puts it in place anyway because it's the only tool that feels severe enough.

5. Depending on the severity (what is taken and for how long) grounding leaves our kids in a position of total loss. In other words, if she has lost her freedom and all her privileges for a month, she has nothing more to lose. This does not encourage cooperation, as there is nothing more to take away. Adding time to the sentence achieves little, since it already feels like forever to our child.

Grounding is also ineffective in the following instances:

- It is used too often.
- It is put out as a threat without follow-through.
- Too much is taken away in one angry swoop. A punishment that is too harsh causes resentment or self-loathing more than learning.

- The parent gives in before the grounding is over. A grounding that is dropped by a soft parent teaches manipulation and weakens our Parent Power.

Despite these drawbacks, this is a tool many parents use regularly as their ultimate weapon and would struggle with losing. It's worth it to see what we can do to make it more of a FREE tool.

To make grounding as functional as possible, take away only the minimum you need to achieve your goal and tell your child what you are doing. "I need you to learn that rude responses are not okay in our house. When you talk that way, I will remove a privilege, starting with the Internet (her favorite item). If you continue, I will move on to television, cell phone, and eventually your freedom (grounding)."

When your child does something you feel is a serious infraction that warrants an immediate grounding, take your time deciding how you will do it. If you feel it calls for removal of all privileges and freedom, give some thought to how this will affect your family before working out the details. Be sure both partners (if applicable) are part of this discussion and that the one who will have to enforce the penalty has the greater input.

Freedom-removal can be accomplished in pieces (an hour/day, evenings, weekends), making it less restrictive yet still effective. Taking time to determine the consequence is better than throwing out an immediate, harsh response in the heat of the moment.

Once you have determined what you are removing and for how long, give some thought to how your child can earn these privileges back. For example, you might ground her for a month and offer to take two days off for every day of *good/helpful* behaviour. Or, for each full week of *good* behaviour she might earn back one privilege (for example, music). This gives her a reason to try, and, while she might ignore this incentive, at least the option is there.

Kids who know they earn back rights for good behaviour are less apt to try to sneak back privileges early and less likely to feel resentful. This allows them to focus on their mistake and lets them know we believe in them despite their error.

In summary, grounding is not a great tool, although there are ways to make it more agreeable. It is difficult to change a primary tool such as this, but it is well worth the effort.

FREE Parenting Tip: Grounding has a lot of drawbacks but, with some creativity, can work successfully. If this is your main parenting tool, you might want to add some new ideas to your parenting pack.

Penalty Called ... Time-Out

A parenting book today would not be complete without mention of time-out. Many of us have used time-out with varying degrees of success. To be effective as a discipline tool, time-out requires a structured approach with a time-out spot, timer, and clearly laid out rules. Unstructured time-outs tend to cause additional problems and challenges.

Some professionals feel time-out, which involves removal from the parent, is damaging to the parent-child bond and can result in increased problems in later years. Others are advocates of this tool and consider it an excellent bottom line to be used whenever a child refuses to do as he is asked.

In my opinion, time-out is neither good nor bad. It is a tool like any other and can be extremely effective in some homes and totally useless or manipulative in others. With the right information and understanding, I think it can be a great tool to have in our parenting pack, even if used only sparingly.

When we talk about time-out, generally speaking we are talking about a process that includes the following guidelines:

- The child is removed from the situation in which the problem behaviour occurred.

- He is not allowed to talk to anyone and no one is talking to him.

- It is a timed event (some use the child's age as the number of minutes the time-out goes for; others use a set time like two minutes). It is the *certainty* of having a time-out and not the amount of time involved that makes it work.

- To be effective, a time-out needs to be consistently and calmly delivered by the parent or adult in charge. Threatening a time-out without follow-through weakens this tool.

A time-out will not work if a child does not care that he is being removed from a situation. For example, if a child is often alone, bored, or lacking stimulation, it will not make any difference to him if he is sent for a time-out. Only an engaging environment is hard to leave, and time-out relies on a child's desire to be around us in order to work.

It can be effective to have varying degrees of time-out. For example, rather than have our child leave the room for a misbehaviour, we might have him stay in the same room, but sit off to the side of the action for a set period of time. If he can't do this without getting attention from others in the room or being disruptive, then we switch him to a removed time-out.

A time-out is rarely a good tool to use when we are really angry at our child's behaviour. Many parents have shared how frustrated they feel when they send their child to time-out and he sits there happily while they are fuming. The parent wants to see remorse or discomfort in the child, and seeing him unfazed by this discipline adds fuel to the fire. Rather than risk a possible overreaction, we are better off to take a time-out ourselves or send our child away, perhaps to his room, until we have calmed down enough to deal with the situation. We might tell our child something like, "I am so angry I can't think straight. Go to your room and we'll talk about it when I'm ready."

Time-Out Alternatives

I am a strong advocate of reserving time-outs for people (adults included) who are losing their self-control and require time to regain their composure. This type of time-out can happen in any room that is close by and empty of people. In this case, I don't mind if the children play, read, sleep, sing—whatever helps them regain control. While they might choose to rant and rave in their isolation, I make it clear that they cannot return from time-out until they have calmed down and are in control. For this type of time-out to be effective, I do not set a timer but instead tell them they can come out when they are ready. If they come out and start to lose it again right away, they go back to time-out for a set minimum time (for example, ten minutes).

Depending on the reason for the time-out, we might ask the child to think about two other ways he could have handled that situation or come up with a way he might "fix" what he has done[25]. He can share these ideas with us when he returns, and a brief discussion of alternative ways to deal with challenges can follow.

> *FREE Parenting Tip: Time-out is a wonderful way to teach kids self-control, however, it can be easy to overuse and raises concerns about what our kids are learning. Time-out also will not help a really frustrated parent— unless the parent takes the time-out herself.*

In her book *Kids Are Worth It!* Barbara Coloroso shares a rule called *You Hit, You Sit.* We applied this rule in our house any time someone hit another person. It meant the person who did the hitting, whether he intended to hurt or not, had to go and sit in a chair by himself and think about what he had done for a set period of time (two minutes). If he was angry, he reserved the right to take a time-out in his room, since this option was always available. When the time was up, the incident was over.

Time-outs in the car or at a restaurant require a bit more creativity and planning. In the car, I let the kids know that their behaviour was not acceptable and used a warning to provide them with a chance to change it. If their behaviour didn't change (or escalated), I'd pull over to the side of the road, turn off the radio, and say, "We're having a time-out. It will start as soon as everyone is quiet." If someone refused to be quiet, I'd assign a further time-out for that person at home and

---

25   This is referring to Diane Chelsom Gossen's *Restitution* model which is all about developing a plan to fix what you have done and come back from the situation strengthened.

add minutes to it until all was quiet. This meant I had to enforce this later at home—no matter how much time had passed or how good that child had been since then!

After a minute, I'd start the car back up and we'd continue on our way. In the car, I'd avoid further discussion of the problem, as that refocuses everyone on what was happening before the time-out and can get the argument going again. Many parents have used this car time-out successfully as their kids seem to respect the seriousness of stopping the car. Of course, this would not be the best tool to use if the kids are dreading their destination or if you are late for an appointment. It is also not the best tool for traveling on public transportation unless the time-out is given after you get off.

In restaurants, stores, doctor's offices, etc, the plan has to be set up and shared in advance to be effective. For example: "We're going to a restaurant for supper tonight. Everyone remember what restaurant behaviour looks like? Excellent! What should we bring to help you be patient while you wait for the food? What will we do if one of us isn't using restaurant behaviour? Where should a time-out happen there?"

If this conversation happens early enough, we might role-play restaurant behaviour and brainstorm ideas about different places in which a time-out could happen (store bench, car, bathroom, at the table) or other possible consequences. At the restaurant, all we need to say is, "Restaurant behaviour, please."

Time-out can be an excellent way to calmly and consistently teach our children. It cannot do everything, but it can be a handy strategy for those times when our child requires a moment to get a grip.

FREE Time-Outs

The main idea behind using time-out is to give the parent a plan to follow that will help her stay calm, controlled, and consistent when her children misbehave. If you find you get angry when using time-out, it might not be the best tool for you.

Before using a time-out, you need to tell your child what it's about, how it will work, what you expect (from both you and your child), and why you're doing it. In deciding on these elements of the time-out, you should take into consideration the age and attention span of your child. The following is one example of how you can present the time-out concept to your child.

"Mommy has a new plan to help us work like a team. It's called time-out, and what it means is if you aren't listening to me or you do something you know you're not supposed to do, you're going to sit by yourself on the chair in the hallway. If you sit quietly, I'll call you after two minutes and you can come back and try things again. I really want to help us learn so we aren't fighting with each other."

Once you have decided to use time-out and explained it to your child, use it. Do not threaten it as this weakens its effect. Use a warning system if you want (that's one … that's two … that's a time-out), but be consistent in its use.

Be fair and recognize that if time-out works with your child, it's because he likes being with you or enjoys being part of a certain activity. If you start nitpicking at everything he does and using a time-out to reinforce your every command, he will stop enjoying your company and start pushing every button he can.

If you put your child in a time-out, wait until he is quiet before starting the clock. Sobbing quietly is okay, but calling you, asking to come out, telling you how angry he is or trying to explain his behaviour is not. Remind him (only once) that he is in time-out and that you will start the clock when he is quiet. Otherwise, ignore him until he is quiet and then start the clock.

When the time-out is over, your child can return to the activity and try again to get it right. If you had asked him to do something (like pick up his toys) and his refusal got him a time-out, get him to come and do it now. Time-out should not be an excuse to get out of undesirable work unless you are willing to set it up that way in advance. "I can see you are too tired to do this. You can take a time-out while I pick up your toys. I'll call you when I'm done, but it might take a while."

As a discipline tool, time-outs are most effective when they are timed events. If you allow the child to come back on his own schedule, he is not learning that sometimes he has to listen to a higher authority.

If, on the other hand, the time-out is being used to regain self-control it is better to have the child determine when he can return to the group. If he comes back early and gets angry again soon after, put a timed piece in place. "I guess you weren't ready to come back out. You go back in for ten minutes, and then I'll check to see if you are ready to rejoin our group."

If your child trashes his room in a time-out, have him clean it up later (as much as possible) and either move the time-out location to an empty space or use a different tool. Another option is to remove most of the things from his bedroom and return them only after he has shown you he can be respectful in time-out. One final option is to overlook the mess (except dangerous items) and simply carry on.

Exercise: Clear Expectations

Of all the things we deal with as parents, perhaps the greatest cause of confusion, hurt, and frustration stems from unknown, unshared, and unmet expectations. Becoming aware of what we expect from others helps us to understand ourselves better and makes it a lot easier for others to understand us. It also helps us see if our expectations are unrealistic and, if so, how unfair we are being by holding on to them. If we neglect to be clear about what we expect from others, we have no right to be angry, hurt, or disappointed when they don't measure up.

Choose an area of your life you currently struggle with and take the following steps:

1. Write the headings of the main people involved in this task across the top of the page (myself, my kids, my spouse, the daycare provider, etc.). Ask yourself, "What are my expectations of (my kids) for this area?" Write down all your expectations under the kids' column then move to the next heading (my spouse). For example, under the heading *My kids* you might write *Helps pack backpack, gets dressed, brushes teeth and hair.*

2. Star those expectations you cannot/will not live without.

3. Put a check beside those that are realistic, fair, and important. For example, while a four-year-old could help wash the floor, it would be unrealistic to think he could do it by himself and unfair to think he would do a nice job. A fourteen-year-old could realistically and fairly be expected to do this job, although perhaps not to your level of expectation. If this job is not important, it does not need a spot on your list.

4. Are any of the starred expectations not checked? If so, can you adapt them to make them realistic and fair?

5. Cross out any expectations that are not starred or checked and let them go.

6. Highlight those still on the list that you have not been clear about to others. Being clear to others means knowing what your expectations are and telling others exactly what you are thinking. If we tell our child to take out the garbage but haven't shared the importance of tying the bag, we have not been clear about our expectations.

7. Go through the list again and develop a plan for sharing your expectations with the people they affect. Are there any you aren't comfortable sharing with others? If so, is it fair to keep them? Decide how important they are to you and either adapt them or let them go.

We can't possibly be aware of every expectation we have for every situation. We can, however, make it a habit to think about what is upsetting us and be clear about our expectations at that moment.

Consider two examples:

"Smarten up or we will leave!" becomes "We play quiet games in a restaurant while we wait for our food."

"You are driving me crazy – stop it!" becomes "I don't like whining, please use your normal voice to talk to me."

We can also spend time thinking about upcoming situations and any expectations we have in that regard. Letting our family know that we expect the dishes done and the counters washed when we return home is much better than walking in the door and attacking them for not having read our mind.

Being clear about our expectations doesn't mean we will always get our way. It does, however, allow us to make our needs known and to understand where our feelings are coming from when things don't go our way. In the end, it makes our reactions that much easier for everyone to understand.

Chapter 10: Working Through Problems

My Learning Chart

My daughter was never a morning person and found getting up and ready for school to be a definite chore. It was at the beginning of second grade when she decided she really didn't need to go to school anymore and began to resist our morning routine. She didn't want to get out of bed and would fight anything and everything about getting ready. She was often late for the bus and once refused to get on it.

This was very hard for me. I started out using my normal strategies of explaining why she needed to comply, giving her as many choices as possible and attempting to build in extra morning time. When those things failed, I moved on to firm directions with consequences and rewards (a treat in her lunch, going to bed earlier, extra story time). I explained that she didn't have to enjoy going to school but that she did have to go.

On the day that she decided she wasn't going out to the bus, I pulled out my Parent Power and began taking things away quickly and forcefully. I knew I had overdone it when I took away her upcoming birthday party! Finally, she went out and got on the bus.

A couple of months into these struggles, I was trained in Triple P, Positive Parenting Program from Australia. In this program, they talked about using behaviour charts as one way to get a child working with you. The idea of behaviour charts was definitely not new to me; in fact, I discussed them quite often in my job at the schools. I did not believe a chart would work in this situation, as my daughter was so strong-willed and very determined not to enjoy this experience. I decided to give it a try just the same.

I created a short list of all the things my daughter needed to get done before getting on the school bus.

Wake up and get out of bed	Make & pack lunch
Get dressed	Eat breakfast
Brush hair	Clean up from breakfast
Wash face	Go to the bathroom
Brush teeth	Out to the bus by 7:40

I wrote those ideas down the left side of the page and the days of the school week across the top. She could check each item off as she did it and earn a star for every day that all things were done. When she had ten stars in a row, I would buy her a book or she could hold on to the stars and when she had twenty I would buy her a ten-dollar Bratz doll. If she wanted to hold out for thirty stars, I would buy her the twenty-dollar doll.

Our morning environment changed immediately. My daughter would get out of bed and run over to the chart and check off that box. Into the bathroom she would go and then come out and check off the appropriate boxes. She continued until all the boxes were checked.

The chart eliminated my nagging, and she was rarely late for the bus again. I bought her one book and one twenty-dollar Bratz doll. By that time, we had been using the chart for a couple months and were able to phase the program out. It was an eye-opener in many ways and really reminded me not to write off tools just because I didn't believe they would work in my family.

What's the Problem?

Dealing with problems is something every one of us has to learn how to face. If people don't teach us how to cope with these challenges, we develop our own methods, although they won't always be healthy. For example, some people cope with a problem by pretending it doesn't exist. They run away, downplay the size or scope of the problem, refuse to talk about it, or use mind-altering substances to try to forget it is there.

This is an interesting idea, since in a previous chapter we noted that things we focus on seem to expand in importance. This suggests the opposite should be true—that if we ignore a problem it should disappear (or at least shrink). There are two things that get in the way of this happening:

1. Even when we are denying there is a problem, we are usually still very aware that it exists. It is not easy to ignore an elephant in the room, and that is often what the problem we're trying to

forget about becomes. As a result, we are giving it brain space, either consciously or subconsciously, and quite likely making it expand.

2. Often problems come with a reality that can't just disappear. A broken window, a teenage pregnancy, a missing dog, these things will not be overlooked. As much as we might want to pretend they didn't happen, the missing window and crunching glass point it out in a very obvious way.

Denying a problem exists does not make it go away. If there is one thing most of us learn as we grow, it's that a buried or downplayed problem has a way of resurfacing and demanding we pay attention to it.

It makes sense to teach our children how to deal with problems in a healthy, productive, and positive way. We start this process by letting our kids know they can always come to us when they have a problem. Self-control and open communication are two important things we must practice to keep this doorway open; they are discussed in chapters 7 and 11, respectively.

The next important piece is to teach our kids the difference between a *problem* and a *reality*.[26] Looking at the situations above, the broken window, the pregnancy, and the missing dog are not the problem, they are the reality. The problems might be the following:

• We live in a climate that requires a window and windows are expensive.

---

26   **Coloroso, p. 101.**

- The girl believes her parents will react badly when they find out she's pregnant and then she'll be on her own.

- The dog belongs to a friend and was in our care.

This is important to understand because if a person focuses only on the reality, it can seem impossible to fix. When things seem impossible to fix, people feel helpless. When people feel helpless they often give up or use desperate measures to solve the problem.

If we take a step back and shift our focus from the reality to the problem, it becomes easier to see possible solutions. We might not feel great about these ideas, but at least we're not helpless.

The next thing to teach our kids is that events are neutral. In other words, there is nothing good or bad about any situation. This means it is our thoughts that make a problem seem insurmountable, not the problem itself. When we are angry, embarrassed, humiliated, or disappointed, our thoughts tend to go in a negative direction, making it difficult to be creative and work out a solution. We need our kids to know that all problems are solvable, no matter how big or uncomfortable they feel at the moment.

FREE Parenting Tip: Problems are a normal part of life. We teach our kids problem-solving skills by modeling them and allowing the kids to help with the process. Problem solving is just a good IDEA.

Finally, our kids should be taught a basic problem-solving model that will help them work through possible solutions and choose which action to take. I like to use the acronym IDEA to help guide me through the process.

Problem-Solving IDEA:

- **I**dentify and define the problem. If you are assisting your child with problem solving, help him to understand the difference between the problem and the unfixable reality.

- **D**evelop a list of ideas to solve the problem; the more ideas you have to solve the problem, the greater your chance of success. Teach your kids to brainstorm and allow every idea to be put on the list (no matter how crazy). Let the person who "owns" the problem do the bulk of the work. As parents, we often take over problem solving, thinking it's our job to come up with ideas for our kids. That is not our role and can create another problem!

- **E**valuate and implement. Look at the choices on the list, and get rid of (or alter) anything that is unreasonable, impossible, or illegal. Choose the best idea from the list of solutions and make a plan for how it will be carried out. Sometimes you will need to flesh out the idea that is chosen.

- **A**ssess how the plan is working and whether or not changes need to be made. Solving a problem will often mean looking back in a day, a week, or a month, to see if things are working. It can be a good idea to state a time in your original plan for when you will go back and evaluate.

A problem is an opportunity for us to learn and to grow. If we model healthy ways to solve problems and involve our children in the process, we are teaching them there is no problem so great it cannot be solved by a good IDEA.

The Captured Toy Box

In the life of a parent, picking things up from underfoot (toys, movies, puzzles) can feel like a never-ending task. It's frustrating at the best of times and downright painful at the worst. Many parents have shared stories of reaching their limit and placing all these precious items into garbage bags to send them off to the garbage, secondhand store, or neighbors' kids. Others hide the toys to teach their kids a lesson.

Usually, when parents get rid of the toys, they regret their rash action and find themselves dealing with guilt and annoyance at having to rebuy the things they gave away. Other times, parents are shocked to learn their children don't notice the missing items or don't seem to care. The parents find themselves dropping hints or making hurtful comments to try to create a feeling of loss or regret for their child.

Parents who hide the toys are even more frustrated when the bags are returned and dumped out with glee. Getting all their things back is like a party to the kids, which wasn't quite what the parent had in mind. In most cases, these parents last less than a day holding the toys hostages and find themselves dealing with yet another big mess for their efforts.

What is a parent to do? We can't be constantly nagging at our children to clean up, and we're not going to run around cleaning up after them. My favorite solution to this problem is one I fondly call the Captured Toy Box.

Creating the Box

Find a box that can fit a fair amount of unloved items. Give the box a catchy name like *Nobody Loves Me Box;* or *Oops, I Forgot Box;* or *Captured Toy Box.* Call a meeting of everyone who will be affected by the box and inform them that from now on any items left out after clean-up time will be "captured"—meaning, put away in the box and not released until a prearranged time.

Once the box is in place, refuse to nag, threaten, or fight about clean-up. You can give a friendly reminder at first ("Captured Toy Box in effect" or "Boy, I hope the box is hungry, there are a lot of things left out still"), but be sure not to make it a habit.

The following are some rules you'll need to think about before starting to capture.

- Who will be allowed to capture things? In our house, my husband and I were both allowed to capture, but I think I took it more seriously than he did.

- When will things be captured? A clear capturing time makes it easier for the kids to get into a routine and decreases the likelihood of adults overusing it. We captured after 8 P.M. when the kids had gone to their rooms for the night. I could have used it to get my kids to clean up before supper by saying capturing will happen at 5 P.M. and again at 8 P.M., but I just used a clean-up song for the 5:00 pick-up and didn't insist we were thorough.

- When will items be released? Choose an actual time for opening the box, and do your best to stick to it. If captured items are in until 1 P.M. Sunday, it doesn't matter how precious the item is, it's in for the duration. Letting things out early will undo the box's purpose and cause no end of badgering for future releases. This is a very important rule that should not be changed unless agreed upon by all when the box is empty.

- When does the box need to be emptied by, and what will happen if it's not? Our box was opened at 1 P.M. and we gave until 7 P.M. on Sunday for everything to be put away. Anything left in after that time was recaptured. If it was recaptured twice, we discussed getting rid of it.

- What will the consequences be for items snuck out of the box early? Come up with an idea that seems fair yet still points out what a serious offence it is. In our house, that item would go to a secluded location for an extra week (although I never needed to use that consequence).

- Will there be consequences for badgering/whining to get your item out early? I gave a resounding yes to this one, as the constant requests would have driven me crazy and undid the benefits of having the box. Any badgering/whining resulted in an extra day's capture after one warning.

- Is there anything that cannot be captured? Make sure everyone knows if certain items are not going to be included in the capturing process. Items required for school, like spelling words, are not great things to capture (although some kids would love it), so use a different strategy for getting those things put away.

- Will there be any exceptions to capturing? On special occasions, I would waive the capture rule until the next day, but otherwise it was always in effect.

When you're ready to start enforcing the box, let everyone know what the rules are and how the capturing will work. Be sure to approach the conversation from a positive standpoint rather than with an *I'll teach you* attitude. If possible, have your family help determine the rules and the consequences for not following them. Allow interested children to decorate the box and put it in a convenient location where people will see it on a regular basis.

Once you've started, if the box gets too full, point out that there are too many unloved items in your house, so some will need to be disposed of or given away. If the box is full because of the size of items being captured, perhaps choosing a larger box would be a better option.

Expect your family to be resistant and test your new limits, especially if you haven't been very consistent in the past. The more definite the consequence the quicker the kids will catch on that you mean business. As well, if the adults in the home are not automatically exempt from the process, the children will buy-in a bit easier.

> *FREE Parenting Tip: The Captured Toy Box is a great way to ensure clean-up is done regularly and without a fuss. It eliminates nagging and provides clear expectations.*

The idea behind the box is to allow you a way to clean up for your kids while still ensuring they are learning something in the process. If you get frustrated when you must pick up after your child and find yourself fuming as you slam-dunk items into the box, then the captured toy box is not going to be the best tool for you.

Finally, remember items are not put in the box as a punishment. If your child does not seem upset by a capture, that's okay. Wait until the release date and see if he puts it away. If he doesn't, then you have a good opportunity to get rid of some clutter.

I have found the Captured Toy Box to be a great way to teach kids about consequences and to instill a sense of responsibility for looking after their own things. Some might argue that in the end we are still picking up after everyone, but it's easy to set things in a box and, because there is a learning piece attached, it just feels right.

Other Ideas for Engaging Kids in Clean-Up

Clean-up will always be easier with our kids if we are clear about our expectations and consequences for when they are not followed. Some other ideas I like to use are the following:

- Make it fun. By far, my favorite strategy for getting young kids to clean up was to make it into a game. I always started with a clean-up song rather than ordering them to come and clean up, which set a nice tone for the job. Sometimes I would pretend I was a cashier and would ask them to bring me four items off the floor to purchase. When they couldn't count, they would grab a few things that I would count for them as I rang it through the pretend check-out. When their items were purchased, I would drop them into the toy box and the kids would run back for more. Other times we put the box in the center of the room and practiced our basket skills by gently throwing the items and trying to get them in the box.

- Provide choices. With young children, you can teach consequences by providing choices. "You can clean up now and I'll help you, or do it later by yourself." If they choose later, you might set a timer (ten minutes) and then remind them to clean up. If they don't, you can put other consequences into effect (item gone for a specified period; they can't take anything else out until that item is put away, etc). If they are tired, the first choice might be "Would you like to clean up, or go rest in your room while Mommy cleans for you?" If they choose the room, you might leave them in there for as long as you feel is required for them to rest (for example, fifteen minutes unless they fell asleep).

- Create limits. If my kids were forming a habit of not helping clean up after crafts or other messy games, I would limit what they could use by saying, "You may bring out the paint, but only if you promise to help clean up after without a fuss. If you don't think you can do that, we'll bring out only one colour today." If we brought it all out and they wouldn't help with clean-up, the next time they could use only one colour.

- Use a timer. When my kids were really involved in an activity and didn't want to clean up as a result, I found it helpful to ask them how much time they needed before they would be able to clean up. Usually they would give me a time like ten minutes (even though they had no concept of time) and I would ask, "If I set the timer for ten minutes will you clean up then without a fuss?" If they agreed, I set the timer and when it went off clean up would start.

As my kids got older my expectations of them increased and, I must confess, the clean-up song stopped. I have clear consequences for any clean-up that doesn't get done now, which I calmly enforce and refuse to argue about. If the person on dishwasher duty forgets to do it, he gets to do it twice in a row. If he forgets a second day, he's on for a week. To make this work, I do not nag or lecture about it, but simply point out when he's failed to do his task. Of course, this same rule applies to us adults as well or it wouldn't work and our kids would likely rebel.

Finally, on cleaning day in our house loose items are put on a bench. By the end of the day, any items left on the bench are considered "left out" and can be claimed by another or thrown away. This doesn't always work, as school textbooks and binders rarely get collected, but at least the pile is all in one spot.

There are many ways we can get our kids to help us clean up, but all of them require us to be patient, calm, consistent and clear. If we can add in creativity in the form of singing, dancing or another fun burst of energy, we've got it made.

The Battle for Bedtime

Putting young kids to bed when they don't feel ready can be challenging. The interruptions by the child as she needs a drink of water, one extra hug, Daddy to lie beside her, or one more story, can leave the parent more exhausted than if he'd let her stay up in the first place. If you have more than one young child going to bed and separate bedrooms, it's even harder.

Part of the problem is that bedtime is one of those areas our children ultimately have the upper hand in; we cannot force them to go to sleep. Our kids cannot force themselves to sleep either, but they can work hard to keep themselves awake. What time our child falls asleep is not something we get to decide, what time they go to their bedroom is. The trick is to get our kids self-monitoring so they recognize when they are tired and need sleep. Eliminating the power struggles that can occur in this area is a much nicer way to end the day.

One way to do this is to develop clear boundaries for our kids and then allow them freedom to work within those boundaries. You can start using this idea as soon as your child moves out of a crib and understands the idea that he must stay in his bedroom. This process will not work with an overtired child, as his reasoning is off, but other times it can be very effective.

It begins by setting up a bedtime routine for the child and then keeping to it as best we can. By doing this, we are helping our child cue their body and create a habit that will help sleep come easier.

Sample routine for an 8:00 bedtime:
7:30—Kids put on pajamas; light healthy snack; brush teeth; read story; hugs and kisses

Choose what time you want your child to be in her bedroom and then begin your routine in advance of that time, if possible. Once your routine is completed, let the child do whatever she needs to do (quietly) to get herself ready for sleep. In other words, rather than insisting lights be out and she lie in bed staring at the ceiling, allow her to do something quietly in her room until she feels ready to sleep. Examples of quiet activities might be: reading, drawing, some floor games (cars, dolls, stuffies), puzzles, some crafts (that don't require washing up after), soft music, etc.

Your child needs to know the options in advance and, whenever possible, help you to create the list of what's allowed. If her activity becomes noisy, a knock on the door or a verbal reminder should be all that's required to quiet her down. If she continues to be noisy, use a stronger reminder: "Can you make this activity work quietly for bedtime or do you need to put it away?" If it gets loud again, the activity is gone and can be discussed in the morning but not that night. In my house, this would mean the child had not cooperated with the bedtime rules and would now need to lie in bed until she could drift off to sleep.

This type of interruption usually happens only once or twice. Once she understands you are serious about the rules, she doesn't want to risk losing her bedtime freedom.

It can be a bit more complicated when kids share a room and one wants to sleep while the other wants to play. This requires a bit more creativity on our part but is still workable. Allowing the awake child to play on the far side of her bed, giving her a reading light, making a blanket fort, or putting in a cheap little tent to play in, are just a few of the options that can be put in place. If they both (all) stay awake, their energy can feed off one another, so be very clear and consistent with follow-through for noise.

The following are some sample rules and critical points to help keep this bedtime routine on track.

- The child may come out of her room only to use the bathroom.

189

- The child may not call the parent to her bedroom unless something really unusual has occurred. I used to allow my kids one call to me and would respond with, "Is this the one important time you need me to come to your room?"

- If a child stays up late and then struggles with getting up on time the next morning, she will need to go into her bedroom a half hour earlier that evening.

- Have a discussion about bedtime rules ahead of time with very clear expectations outlined. It might take work to be clear on what is acceptable, but that will make things go much more smoothly.

- Expect a child who has been fighting with you at bedtime to really test for consistency. She will be looking for the loopholes that will make you engage in a power struggle. You know your child better than anyone else, so be sure to take her tendencies into account when choosing the time to set. Make it work for both of you.

This routine can help our kids learn to self-monitor and help us avoid power struggles at bedtime. It is critical we stay calm throughout the process and be consistent with our rules. Role-model your own self-awareness to your child: "Boy, I'm really tired tonight. I think I'll go to bed early" and avoid nagging or blaming.

The idea for this bedtime routine came to me because I can lie in bed for hours staring at the ceiling just wishing sleep would come. It can be very uncomfortable and makes me, an in-control adult, want to cry out in frustration. Most sleep programs will tell you that if you can't sleep, get up and do something to empty your brain and allow your body to shut down and get ready to sleep.

Having our kids fall asleep easily isn't about our convenience. By teaching them how to prepare for rest (having a before-bed routine), how to unwind (by doing quiet activities), and how to self-monitor (recognize when they are tired), we are creating bedtimes that can be pleasant for everyone.

> *FREE Parenting Tip: Providing our kids with a bedtime routine that allows them to self-monitor and sleep when they are ready cuts down on power struggles and other issues.*

Taking Tantrums off the Menu

Mealtimes are often challenging for parents of young children. What's supposed to be a time of connecting and sharing becomes a time of tears and argument instead. It is a common time for power struggles, as the parent wants to call the shots and say *what* the child should eat (or *that* the child should eat), and the child subconsciously recognizes this as an area he can control.

This chapter provides ideas to make mealtimes more enjoyable and less battle-prone for families that find this an issue. Barbara Coloroso's book *Kids Are Worth It!* provides plenty of ideas to help remove the emotion from the dining experience and replace it with positive connection and self-awareness. When my kids were young, I took these ideas, adapted them to fit my family, and had a much happier mealtime experience as a result.

One way to make sure mealtimes are pleasant experiences is to allow your child to help choose the meal. Set some healthy boundaries and then allow him to choose, "Do you want chicken or hamburger tonight?" If he can't or won't decide, do not stress over it. Simply change to something like, "I'm going to choose chicken for tonight. Do you want the carrots cooked or raw?" You don't have to let the child choose the whole meal, but the more you include him the greater the chance that he will decide to eat it.

Let your child choose how much food is put on his plate. Often, the adults at the table will ladle out the portions for everyone. This can be the cause of many problems. We can't possibly know how hungry our kids are or even how much they like that food. By having our child determine how much he wants, we are teaching him to tune in to his body and monitor how he feels.

Since he is just starting to learn how portions work, there are a few things we should keep in mind so we can make it a positive experience for everyone:

1. If the child really likes to scoop, he might take more than he can eat. In that case, limit the amount to one scoop and let him know he may have another when he's finished his first. If he really likes scooping, perhaps you can let him scoop out some for the adults in the house (or other agreeable children).

2. If the child loves the meal and would empty the pan without thought of what others will eat, a limit must be set. This is a good opportunity to teach your child about sharing and being polite by being clear on the number of pieces each has to start.

3. When the child wants only two peas but half the tray of french fries, problems could arise. When this happens, you might teach him about nutritional balance by saying something like, "One scoop of peas balances one scoop of french fries." If he really doesn't like peas, you might ask what vegetable he would prefer to balance out his fries. If he chooses another, have him go to the fridge (if he is able) and get the new food rather than interrupting your meal for his special "extras."

4. In some cases, you might want to have a rule like, "Everyone needs to try a little bit of everything." I tell my kids that you never know when your taste buds are going to change. What a shame it would be to live half your life thinking you hate something only to find out later your tastes have changed. Our children's palates are forming as they grow. The more variety we offer, the more chance they have of developing a wide range of tastes.

5. When having a meal you know your child will try one bite of and then refuse to eat, it is a good idea to have a backup plan. One way to deal with this is by telling your child he can get himself something else to eat providing it is healthy—but make sure you discuss food qualifications for this rule before you put it in place. Since you've already created a meal, your child should make this one on his own and clean up whatever mess he makes while getting it. When my kids were young, they would choose something like fruit and yogurt that didn't require any cooking. Alternatively, he could wait until you are finished eating for help with cooking something.

6. If your child scoops his own food and then chooses not to eat it all, you need a clear and consistent rule about what will happen. For example, "If you don't want to eat what you've put on your plate, you may wrap it up. If you are hungry between now and bed, you may eat that first before having anything else." This provides him with a variety of options, such as the following:

    -   He might go to bed without eating what was on his plate or anything else.
    -   He might head back to his plate later (when he is really hungry) and devour it.
    -   He might return and eat part of his food.

    You decide if there will be any flexibility to your rule. If he was warned he was taking too much, then your rule might be unbending. If he made a good effort but simply misjudged how filling the meal would be, you might decide to let it go as a learning experience.

Self-awareness is a critical piece of healthy living and an important skill for our children to have. As our kids learn to think about their meals, they become better able to judge when and what to eat. Mealtime should not be about tears and arguments. The more we allow our children to listen to their body's messages and respect what they hear, the more we allow our mealtimes to become a time of positive sharing and connecting.

FREE Parenting Tip: Mealtimes can be a source of stress for families. The more we allow our kids to make decisions based on their own self-awareness, the more we reduce mealtime stress and increase family togetherness.

Exercise: Creating a Good IDEA

Many of the ideas shared in this book are things I have made up to make my life with my kids easier. I'm not especially gifted at creativity ... just really motivated. With this exercise, I challenge you to choose a topic you battle over on a regular basis in your house and develop a creative, workable solution. I've used my IDEA problem-solving model with a few extra steps built in, but feel free to use whatever structure will be most helpful to you.

I. Identify the situation you are trying to solve:
For example: kids refusing to take their turn exercising the family dog

_____

_____

_____

_____

Expectations of all involved:
For example: Mom is willing to walk the dog every morning but expects the others in the family to take a turn and give the dog 45 minutes of exercise each evening.

_____

_____

_____

_____

D. Develop a list of possible solutions. Write down any and all solutions that are proposed without analysis. Try to come up with at least ten.
For example:
1. *Mom continues to walk the dog a.m. and p.m. but does not contribute to supper preparations or clean-up*

2. *A schedule is created and rotated through, with each person taking his turn*

3. *A dog-walker is hired to walk the dog in the evening, and the money to pay is taken from the family fun money or kids' allowances*

E. Evaluate the list of solutions and choose the best. Look at the list of options and delete any that are illegal, impossible, immoral, or infuriating. In other words, go through and make sure the ideas that are kept are realistic, possible, legal, and fair. If none are left, start the process over. Blend remaining ideas to come up with one that makes sense and everyone can agree with.

For example: A rotating schedule will be set up for the evening walk with all taking turns. Whoever is on dog duty will not need to take part in supper preparation or clean up.

Discuss consequences for noncompliance and set a date for follow-up. Remember that a consequence is not a punishment but rather a logical response to an action (or inaction)

For example: If the dog has not been walked by 7:00 P.M., Mom will walk her and charge the appropriate person a fee of $____ (or other prearranged exchange) for dog-walking duties.

Consequences:

_____

_____

_____

_____

A. Assess how it worked. Set a follow-up date.

_____

If a rule is not followed, put consequences in place calmly and consistently. At follow-up, decide if and how the plan needs to be adapted to fit the needs of your family.

Chapter 11: Are We Communicating?

My Do-Over Option

Over the years, I have learned quite a variety of parenting techniques, especially around communication skills. I teach on these topics often and do my best to practice what I preach. Despite this, I definitely have moments when I do not use my skills properly. I might give a rude or snappy reply, or maybe behave in a way that makes the situation worse than it needed to be. Sometimes, I even recognize what I am doing and still continue doing it.

I'm not sure why I do this, but I have figured out that I am not the only one who does it. In fact, I find parents are often relieved to hear that I do it too. This got me thinking about my kids and how they sometimes make a rude statement, use a tone that communicates disrespect, or snub me with a look. I decided if I can know all that I teach and still choose to behave poorly, perhaps I need to cut them some slack and provide them opportunities to practice positive behaviour before pulling out a consequence.

As a result, I came up with the idea to offer my kids an opportunity to rewind and try a second time when their words, look, or tone of voice were leading them into trouble. The way this works is if my kids speak in a disrespectful or irritating way, (i.e., whining), I ask them if they would like to try that again. I'm careful to say this in a nonjudgmental voice (which can be hard to do when my child just suggested I am the stupidest person alive) to ensure my offer doesn't come across as a threat.

The purpose of doing this is to give my kids a chance to practice their skills and make them super aware of what disrespect looks and sounds like. If they continue being disrespectful, consequences are put in place.

Here are some examples to illustrate how it works.

Example #1:
Child: Mom, where's my backpack?
Mom: I don't know. I never used it. Where did you last have it?
Child (sneering voice): If I knew that I wouldn't be asking.
Mom: Would you like to try that again?
Son (nicer voice): I don't know where my backpack is—that's why I'm asking.
Mom: I haven't seen it, but you might check the back closet.

In this situation my child self-corrected immediately, and we carried on as if the sneering voice hadn't happened.

Example #2:
Child (making a disgusted face): Chicken again! I hate chicken!
Mom: Would you like to try that again?

Child: I think I've had enough chicken. I'll make myself something else to eat.

Mom: That's fine.

It is tempting in this situation to add on a lecture about how difficult it is to come up with supper ideas and about appreciating my effort, but if I did that it would defeat the purpose.

Example #3:

Mom: Time to turn off the computer. Why don't you go outside for a while?

Child (whining): I don't want to go outside—it's hot out there. Why do I have to turn off the computer?

Mom: I can't hear whining ... do you want to try that again?

Child (loudly): I don't want to go outside ... it's hot!

Mom: I could certainly hear that, but it didn't feel any better. Computer is off for the afternoon. If you want to stay inside, you can empty the dishwasher.

In this case my child did not correct his behaviour but simply changed it to another undesirable response. As a result, he got a minor consequence and a choice. If he still didn't correct his behaviour he might have an additional consequence added in (perhaps computer gone for the rest of the day and *required* to empty the dishwasher).

Disrespect is not always easy to identify when you are the one being disrespectful. Sometimes you are simply letting your feelings show and are not aware those feelings are surfacing in such a rude way. I believe we can all use a do-over once in a while. Our kids need to test our boundaries (especially as they get older), and they require lots of opportunities to practice their self-control. This little trick saves me from lots of unnecessary battles and allows my children plenty of opportunities to practice their skills.

What Did You Call Me?

Name-calling is a common occurrence with children, whether they have siblings or not. Some of it is in good fun and some is downright hurtful. I think it is important we raise our kids to understand they are resilient enough to deal with name-calling, while at the same time (partly for our own sanity) have a way to discourage this troublesome behaviour.

If you are not bothered by your children calling each other names, then you need not do anything about it. Before writing it off entirely, however, let me caution you about one thing: there is a difference between teasing and hurtful putdowns. The first is meant to be fun. Done properly it actually builds the relationship between those involved as it usually makes them laugh and creates a positive connection. It is not meant to hurt, and when the person being teased gets upset, the teaser apologizes or at least stops the teasing. Perhaps the most important quality of this kind of teasing is that the comments can go both ways, with the role of teaser and teased shifting between those involved.

Insults, on the other hand, are meant to put a person down and are a different story altogether. They are meant to hurt and are often aimed at something a person is sensitive about. The teaser does not stop when their target becomes upset, but actually increases the taunts. There is usually a power imbalance (age, size, authority), which results in the insults flowing in one direction as the person being teased believes he will be hurt worse if he tries to give it back. This type of teasing can be done openly or secretly and, once it starts, will often get worse without adult involvement. This can be a first step toward bullying and is worth doing something about. Even when it's not headed for bullying, it can be hard on the self-esteem and can cause major (lifetime) rifts in relationships.

Despite this, kids are extremely resilient and should be taught how to stand up for themselves rather than rescued from most situations. Sympathy for a person who is feeling victimized is not useful. We help our kids by providing them with skills, not by rescuing.

My goal was to teach my kids how to joke with each other without truly hurting. It's not that I didn't feel my kids were strong enough to handle the hurt, but more that I wanted them to be building a relationship that would stick with them throughout their lives. The fact that I dislike listening to bickering and arguing provided an extra incentive to come up with a plan for dealing with name-calling.

Name-Calling Rule: *If you call someone a name (insult, putdown, etc.), you must say two nice things about that person to help build him or her back up.*

This rule was put in force when my children were very young (about three years old) and applied to every one of us. Terms of endearment (sweetie, honeybunch) were okay, as long as the person being called those names was okay with it. To make the rule easier, anytime a person was called something other than his or her name, a foul could be called. At first, it shocked me when I was called to task for affectionately calling my son a turkey. Then, I realized that if it offended him I needed to know about it.

If a person was called something and requested *two nice things,* the rule was in effect, no questions asked. Other people could also call for two nice things if they witnessed a name-calling, but in the end it was up to the target to determine if a "buildup" was required. If a person refused to say two nice things, or argued that no offense had occurred ("I was only joking, that's not name calling"), the number increased to four. If he continued to resist, the number went to six and he was sent away from the group to come up with his compliments. He could return when he had come up with his six compliments and was ready to share them.

If the name-calling occurred in front of others, the compliments were done that way as well. This decreased any desire to call a sibling a name to look cool in front of friends and then tell her in private that she really is great and he likes being around her.

When my kids were young and just learning this rule, I would offer to help them come up with the compliments. I did this both so I could model what a good compliment sounded like and because sometimes it is hard to think of nice, original things to say. To cut down on repeat offenses, we insisted that you could not use the same compliment twice in one day and things like *Sorry* or *I love you* did not qualify as compliments.

FREE Parenting Tip: A good, clear rule telling our kids they must say two nice things about anyone they decide to call a name can decrease insults and build self-esteem.

Sample compliments may include the following:

You're fun to play with	You're nice
You make good Lego creations	You're very patient
You make great forts	You give great hugs
You tell great stories	You're funny
You're very creative	You're a good cook
I like being around you	You're helpful

Of course, the compliments would change with age, but in our house I found it was the insults that seemed to completely disappear. "What did you call me?" is something I rarely hear in my house today, and, for the most part, name-calling really is in good fun.

Connecting through Conversation

Empathic listening is a tool that helps people hear what another person is telling them and build connection at the same time. To do it correctly, we must imagine ourselves in the other person's situation and try to relate to how they are feeling. It must be done with open ears, mind, and heart. Our goal is to detach from our own feelings and work on understanding the feelings of the other person. This can be challenging if what we are hearing affects us as well, but it is a key factor in getting the whole story.

The strategy for empathic listening involves the following steps:

- Listen to what the other person has to say and focus fully on him.
- Empathize. Try to think about how that person might be feeling and share these thoughts with the speaker.

- Reflect back what you have heard, and clarify if necessary.
- Assist with problem solving ONLY if requested to do so.

Here is one example of empathic listening that involves a child's emotional outburst.

Child: I hate Grandma!
Parent: You sound angry. What's going on?
Child: Grandma's mean, she never plays with me.
Parent: Hmm, I don't think I'd like it if my grandma never played with me, especially if she used to play with me a lot.
Child: Yeah. Now she's always busy with the baby.
Parent (nodding): So, do you think the problem is that's she's spending too much time with the baby?
Child: Yeah. Can I have a cookie?

There are two important points here.

1. Getting past the strong opening statement the child made can be a hurdle for many parents. Those are potent words, and if we want to find out where they are coming from we have to ignore our own emotions and listen for our child's.

2. The child ended the conversation without asking the parent to help fix the problem. Parents love to fix problems, even when they are not asked to do so. In this case, and in more cases than you might imagine, the child just needed to be heard. His feelings were making him uncomfortable, resulting in his strong opening statement. At some point, he might bring it up with his parent again and ask for help with ideas, but if not,

it is far more empowering for him if the parent just allows the conversation to end there.

Here is an example of empathic listening with a bullying disclosure.

Child: "I pretended to be sick because Bart said he was going to bash my head in and teach all the wimps at school a lesson!"
Parent: "Wow, that sounds pretty scary."
Child: "I'm not scared, I'm mad!"
Parent: "Okay, mad makes sense too. If it were me, I think I'd be both mad and scared."
Child: "I guess I am kind of scared. Could I stay home tomorrow too?"
Parent: "I wish I could let you. I don't think I would want to go back either. I think the school might get upset though."
Child: "They won't care. You can just tell them I'm sick."
Parent: "You know what Bart is doing is *not* okay. He has no right to treat you or anybody like that. What he's doing is bullying. How about we come up with a plan to help you work through this problem?"

In this case, the parent raises the idea of problem solving together. Bullying is a serious issue that arises only when there is a power imbalance of some sort. Often our kids will need some guidance to work their way through it. If the child responded by saying "No. I'll deal with it myself," the parent could agree but end with a *check-back* statement. "Okay, how about I check in with you again on the weekend to see how it went?" The result would be a child who feels supported, cared for, and empowered by his parent's belief in his ability.

Sometimes we have trouble identifying the name of the feeling and, in fact, the speaker himself might not be clear how he feels. Don't get caught up in identifying the feeling or it could become a circus (for example, "Are you mad?" "No." "Irritated?" "No!" "Frustrated?" "**No!**" "Furious?" "**NO!**") The idea is to connect with the person by trying to understand his feeling. Guessing it right is not that important. We will never truly know what's going on inside another person. If he says he is not angry, despite his clenched jaw, red face, and throbbing temple, accept it and move on.

Finally, sometimes our child will not be receptive to us, even though we use this communication tool perfectly. If that's the case (you can tell because he is escalating instead of calming), ditch this tool and move into self-preservation. Calmly say something like "I can see you're not ready to talk about this now. Let me know if you want to talk later." Then walk away and refuse to engage in further argument.

> *FREE Parenting Tip: Empathic listening helps us to connect with our kids and helps them feel heard and understood. Practice using it on a regular basis and watch your relationship grow.*

Communicating Our Underlying Message

We all know the way we talk has an influence on how other people respond. What we might not be totally aware of is that the words we say are only a small piece of the message we send. Our body language and tone of voice play a big role in communication and often speak louder than words.

Having said that, I find that by becoming aware of the words you are using and really thinking about the message you want to send, your body language and tone will often follow suit. All in all, becoming aware of what and how you say things can make a huge difference in the relationships you build.

Let's take a look at some of the more common pitfalls parents fall into while keeping in mind that the kindest words in the world can become rude with a simple roll of the eyes or change in tone.

Bossing: "Put your books away and come to the table! "
Meeting the child's statements with disbelief: "The teacher yelled at you *for no reason?*" (eyebrows raised)
Telling the child how she feels: "You must be cold—it's cold out here. Put on your jacket."
Using a certain tone: "Jay-SON!"
Telling the child what she likes: "You do so like grapes. Eat them."
Misusing Parent Power: "You'll do it and you'll like it, or your play station is gone!"

These modes of communication might not sound like a big deal, and, in fact, you might be thinking these practices sound like everyday parenting. You are right—they are very common. But imagine what these practices feel like to our kids. To help parents understand this better, during my parenting sessions I often have a few volunteers pretend to be my dinner guests. I set a table and have them start by arriving at my door. I greet them enthusiastically with something like, "Welcome, it's good to see you. Quick, shut the door, you're letting in all the bugs!" I insist they wash up before coming to the table and smell their hands to see if they used soap. Throughout the meal, I ask them questions, cut them off to correct their behaviour, and hand one of them a tissue in the middle of his story and insist he wipe his nose.

In other words, I treat my guests as if they are children and then talk to the whole group about how it felt. Without fail, the volunteers are surprised at how frustrated or rebellious they felt during the process.

One minute I was friendly and fun, the next I was telling them what to do in a way that made them feel foolish.

Respect is taught through our actions and words. If we want our children to be respectful, we need to model how it is done. We can't teach respect by treating them disrespectfully, even though it might seem more efficient.

Here are some good communication methods to build respect and self-esteem in your child:[27]

- ***Ask* for things to be done.** "Will you please put your books in your room?" Alternatively, *describe* a situation and let your child figure out what needs to be done. "Your books are on the dinner table."

- **Provide *choices* or *set expectations*.** (And then try not to nag). "Are you going to move your books, or would you like to peel the potatoes (make supper, set the table) while I move them?" Another option that Faber and Mazlish share in *How to Talk So Kids Will Listen and Listen So Kids Will Talk,* is to make your request and then leave a note. For example, "Your books need to move before you use the computer." A note on the computer keyboard might read, *Please move me first—Your Books.*

- **Give your child the *benefit of the doubt*.** "Your teacher yelled at you for no reason. That must have been confusing." This

---

27   Excellent examples of how to communicate respectfully can be found in the books *How to Talk So Kids Will Listen and Listen So Kids Will Talk* and *Tongue Fu* (see Suggested Reading)

statement must reflect that you believe what your child has said, so be careful not to sound sarcastic or roll your eyes.

- **Use *active or empathic listening* to flesh out the story.**
Listen, clarify, and recognize feelings (empathize). Use as calm a tone as you can muster and be aware of your body language. Avoid giving advice unless asked. For example,
Parent: Your teacher yelled at you for no reason? That must have been confusing.
Child: She's so mean. I hate her.
Parent: I think I would be angry if someone did that to me.
Child: I was embarrassed.
Parent: I can understand that. So, then what happened?

- **Save *"no"* for when you really mean it.** For example, when it doesn't have to be a "no" try "Maybe,"; "Convince me"; "Yes, later"; "Tell me more"; "Let me think about that"; or "I'm not sure that's going to work, but I'm open to hearing more." When you must use "no" be sure you can provide a good reason for it.

FREE Parenting Tip: How we communicate with our children should reflect how we want them to talk to others. We model respectful communication by demanding less, giving our child the benefit of the doubt, and by being a good listener.

Even respectful communication will sometimes fail to meet the mark, and your child will respond with rude behaviour. When this happens, try to be the bigger person and calmly restate your request. You will make mistakes—we all do. Thankfully, our kids give us lots of opportunity to practice.

Keeping Communication Flowing

When our kids are little, they tell us things without regard for consequence to themselves or others. As they grow, they begin to learn that some things they say result in undesirable reactions from adults and might be better left unsaid.

From the parent's perspective, we want our kids to trust us enough to share big things like telling on someone who's planning to do something dangerous, talking about drug/alcohol use, turning in a bully, or confessing to serious mistakes. How we react to this news is going to influence how comfortable they will be telling us things in the future.

If we want our kids to share with us, we need to make sure we are not slamming the door in their face when they come to us to talk.

Common Door-Slammers

Overreact	"I knew you did it!" or "This is serious. I'm phoning the school first thing tomorrow and demanding they do something about this!"
Demand answers	"Who did it? Tell me so I can let the coach know!"
Threaten	"Tell me the truth right now or you are grounded forever!"
Use sarcasm	"What do you mean it was an accident? Your fist just swung out all on its own?!"

By the time our kids are three to four years old, the first inklings of self-preservation start to limit what they are willing to share. If a parent asks a child if he wrote on the wall and he is punished when he confesses, he has learned that telling the truth doesn't feel very good. If, on the other hand, he lies and gets out of it by saying his one-year-old sister did it, he has learned that telling a lie is worth it. In other words, if there is no benefit to telling the truth, our child might as well lie and hope he is never found out.

By seven to eight years old, the social code for turning in others has been learned. This is the age when our kids' sense of self-worth starts to shift from a family focus to more dependence on peers. The unspoken code comes through clearly—ratting on a classmate, a bully, or a friend can have very negative consequences. Being picked on, left out, or beaten up for telling on someone is a good reason to keep your mouth shut.

Our goal as parents is to open that door to communication as wide as we can so our toddlers and teenagers feel comfortable talking to us about problems big and small. We can do this by allowing the following principles to guide us and teaching them to our children:

- Telling the truth will always be rewarded in some way.

- There is a difference between tattling (ratting), which is getting someone into trouble, and telling or getting someone out of trouble or danger.

- When you take a risk and share sensitive information with me, I (the parent) will do all I can to help and support you in return.

We can further reinforce these messages by staying calm when the words we are hearing are driving us nuts. Door-openers must be said using a calm, nonjudgmental voice and manner or they will not have the desired effect.

Good Door-Openers

Encourage information	"I wonder if you're trying to protect your friend. That's very loyal of you and I respect that. This is serious stuff, though, and something will have to be done. How about you tell me the rest and then we'll come up with a plan together?"
Stay calm	"Thank you for telling me the truth. I know that was hard, and I will take it into account when I'm coming up with a consequence."
Clarify	"Let's see if I understand this right. You were playing, and he just ran right into your fist, and he thought you punched him? Were you guys talking before that?"

A simple guideline I like to use is, "Am I being respectful? Would I talk this way to a friend or colleague?" If not, how else could I say it? On occasion I have to remind my kids to be respectful to me, and other times it's my kids giving me the reminder, "You might not like it, Mom, but at least it's the truth!"

Sometimes, despite our having a great open relationship with our kids, they will neglect to share something we think is worthy of mention. If this happens, try not to be offended and instead use it as a teachable moment. Let your child know that this would have been a good thing to share. It's not always easy to know what falls on the "sharing" list.

When it comes to sharing tough stuff, we all need to be clearly heard. The safer we make this environment for our kids, the more likely the conversation will happen. People always have a reason for doing the things they do. If we can keep communication flowing by really trying to understand our children's point of view, we are opening an important door in our parenting world.

FREE Parenting Tip: Keeping our kids talking to us requires an atmosphere of trust, predictability, and support—all created using open-door communication.

Stand Up and Be Counted

Being assertive is about saying what you need to say rather than keeping it bottled up inside or allowing it to explode aggressively all over the other person. It requires tact, personal strength, and clarity of what you believe.

It is important when being assertive to understand that this is something we do for ourselves so we can feel good and let go of negative emotions. It is not about getting our way or setting the other person straight, but about saying our piece and feeling good about ourselves in the process. Understanding this is important. If we think being assertive is about changing someone else's behaviour and he doesn't change, we might feel our assertiveness failed. We can't control other people. If our success relies on other people changing their behaviour, life will be very disappointing.

Interestingly, one of the great things about being assertive is that the offender is often counting on our passive reaction (doing nothing) or our aggressive reaction (attacking). When we assertively respond with strength and composure, it can throw the offender off balance and result in a change in his behaviour. It can even create a reluctant form of respect and may result in permanent changes in his behaviour toward you. When this happens, we should consider it a bonus, as we reap the rewards of our honesty and witness a positive result from our actions.

If you are already practiced at being assertive, teach the skill to your child by role-modeling it often. If, like many people, you have gotten this idea confused with aggression or have become submissive to make life easier, it's a good idea to develop your own skills before concerning yourself with your child's. Remember, our kids learn more from what they see us do than from what we tell them.

Another option is to work on this skill together. Role-playing with our kids can be a great way to practice and have some fun.

Being Assertive

Stance: when I work with students, I have them practice their assertive body by pretending they are wearing a cape and a crown. I explain that their shoulders and head need to be held in a strong, confident position to pass for royalty, and that's exactly what the assertive stance should look like. Shoulders should be up and back (a slight puffing of the chest, if you will), while the head is held high and proud. Lowering of the head in a submissive gesture will cause our crown to topple to the ground, while raising our nose to indicate superiority will make it slip backwards.

Hands should be relaxed at our sides. Fists suggest anger and send a message to both our brain and the other person that a fight is looming. Crossed arms tend to indicate defensiveness or fear. It's okay to put your hands in your pockets, but be sure to display strong shoulders if you do this.

Facial Expressions: Becoming aware of your facial expressions when you are angry, afraid, embarrassed, or confident is an important part of being assertive. This is best practiced in front of a mirror so you can see what confidence looks like and rehearse using that face in private. If you look aggressive (angry) or submissive (afraid) when you are standing up for yourself, things will likely not go the way you had planned. Once you believe you're able to do it, try it out with people you trust so they can give you their feedback.

Eyes: Your eyes are also an important part of assertiveness. Be sure to look at yourself in the mirror during practice and get used to how looking someone in the eye feels. In real situations, you can shift your gaze to the other person's forehead or nose if looking him right in the eye is too much. Unless it is respectful in your culture to avert your gaze, you cannot look at the floor or the ceiling and appear confident, so be sure to get a grip on those eyes.

Voice: Being assertive means standing up for something important to you, and that needs to be reflected in your voice. You do not need to sound friendly, but you should not sound angry or afraid either. Take a deep cleansing breath before you begin talking to ensure that your voice comes out strong and true. Remember that you are royalty at this moment; use a voice that matches that confident authority.

Words: What you say when you are being assertive is going to make a difference. If you use attacking words your opponent will likely attack back. Your goal is to get your message across and stand up for what you believe in without causing a battle or putting the other person down.

This means you will have to know what your message is (what it is you're standing up for) and practice saying things in ways that support your message. Starting sentences with a statement about your own feelings is less attacking for the other person.

Examples:

"I don't like being spoken to in a rude way."
"I believe what I have to say is important. Please let me finish."
"I don't appreciate people sitting on the hood of my car—get off it, please."
"I can see you guys are excited about the party, so go. I'm staying here."
"I can't concentrate with this yelling; please quiet down so we can talk."
"I see you're angry. I'll give you time to calm down before we talk."

Assertiveness does not have to be done using "I" statements, but it works better if we at least think that way to figure out what we are feeling and why. Once we have the information about our feelings, we could change the format to something like, "This isn't working for me. When you yell, I can't concentrate. Please stop so we can talk."

Polite words (*please, thank you, excuse me*) are not required in assertive statements, but sometimes they just feel right. If you choose to add them in, make sure they don't come out in a pleading way, because that will undermine what you are trying to do. You also should be aware that using manners in a situation like this can create a sense of moral injustice for you if the offender responds rudely (*how dare he still treat me rudely after I said please!*).

If the person doesn't do as you've asked, you might choose to leave the situation, go for help, or turn your attention to something else. If you allow negative thoughts or feelings to play over and over in your mind, you are doing more harm to yourself than the offender ever could have done. Stand up and be counted, then let it go. That's assertiveness at its best.

> *FREE Parenting Tip: Assertiveness is a skill that must be done with your crown and cape firmly in place. It's about standing up for yourself without putting others down and about feeling good as a result of your efforts.*

Exercise: Being a Good Listener

Really listening when our kids are talking to us can be a challenge. When we are not caught up in our own thoughts and only half listening, we are often tempted to make jokes about the things we hear, ask questions that make the conversation diverge onto a different path, or try to guess the outcome before it is delivered. All of these things interrupt the storyteller and make sharing the story much less fun.

If you haven't been practicing active listening and have been getting into the habit of any (or all) of the above, it's a good idea to go back to the basics and remind yourself how to be a good listener. Here are some ideas to help you do that.

1. When your child comes to you with a story about her day, set aside whatever you are doing and give her your full attention. If you are in the middle of something you can't put aside, tell her you really want to be able to give her story your full attention and ask if you could continue the conversation at a specific time.

    "This sounds like an important story and I would really like to give it my full attention. Can we talk about it in ten minutes when supper is in the oven?"

2. Look at your child, make comfortable eye contact, and allow her to talk.

   "Okay, I'm ready. Let's hear what you wanted to tell me."

3. Show you are listening through your body language (still focusing on the speaker) and by giving verbal feedback once in a while.

   "Hmm; wow; interesting; go on; I see," while the head is nodding.

4. Check that you understand what your child is saying by clarifying pieces when required. Be sure to clarify, not make assumptions or take over the story.

   "So, you and the twins were down in the basement with the dog?"

5. Listen until she has finished her story and then comment.

   "Wow, that sounds like quite an adventure…thanks for sharing."

Active listening might sound like common sense, but often it's these simple skills that get buried in our parenting pack and easily forgotten or overlooked. Challenge yourself to practice this skill for a full week and see if you notice a difference in how much your child is sharing.

Part 4

Caring for the Caregiver

Chapter 12: Controlling Our Personal Pressure

My Time-Out Penalty

One of my favorite stories to share with parents is about a situation when my kids were playing unsupervised on the main floor of my house while I was preoccupied upstairs. My son was a preschooler at the time and my daughter a toddler, so why I left them alone for so long is beyond me (about half an hour). I think I called down the stairs a couple times to make sure both were still breathing, but I know I didn't go down there to check.

When I did go downstairs, I found a trail of squished, brown muffin pieces strewn across my white (previously clean) linoleum that continued down into the family room. Walking further into the kitchen, I came across a stool covered in the remainder of the muffin and more on the floor around it. I let out a cry of frustration as my sock stuck to the floor from what I could only guess was spilled apple juice. Looking around, I could see glistening little puddles everywhere. I could also see my kids in the living room happily playing so I headed in there to confront them.

My son launched into his story, "Mommy, I got breakfast for me and, and, and, Lissa. Muffins, and, and juice and, and, and some apples and … " As he excitedly told his story, his drinking box, which he held in his hand, moved back and forth shooting juice on the carpet.

I couldn't take it any longer. "Stop," I screamed, "just stop! You are getting juice everywhere. What a mess you two have made!"

My son stopped talking. With a shocked look on his face, he set down his juice, put his hands on his hips, and, in a firm voice said, "Mommy, I think you need a time-out." Looking at him standing there so confident and sure, I instantly knew he was right. I nodded my head, turned on my heels, and went into my bedroom for a time-out.

Tears came to my eyes as I sat on my bed repeating my parenting mantra[28] and feeling yet again like I had failed. After a couple minutes, I heard my kids whispering outside my door. A moment later, there was a gentle knock. "If you are calm now, you can come out," my son said. "And if you need a hug, Lissa and I have one for you."

I accepted that group hug and then apologized to my kids for losing my cool and yelling at them. We cleaned up the mess together and dedicated the rest of the morning to play time. It was a learning experience for all three of us, and one I fondly share with others.

---

28   **My parenting mantra is: "I'm a great mom; I'm lots of fun; I keep my cool; Cause that's my rule." I try to picture myself relaxed and playing with my kids while repeating this over and over aloud or in my mind.**

Be the Elastic

Stress is a necessary and important part of living effectively. If you picture an elastic band in a drawer, you'll notice it lacks a reason for being. That elastic has the ability to do a lot of things, but not without stress. Stress is what gets that band moving— it provides purpose and direction. This analogy can help us see that stress is a useful and necessary force in our world, although since an elastic band lacks free will, it is totally at the mercy of the person using it.

Similar to the elastic, if we commit to too many things at once, or get pulled in too many directions, we are in danger of snapping. Yet, how many of us over commit? We take on too much or don't allow for extra struggles in our life and then act surprised when we can't handle the pressures. For instance, life transitions (moving, marriage, babies, loss, etc.) naturally increase stress in our lives, stretching our limits and decreasing what we can comfortably take on. Yet, when we are going through a major transition, we rarely recognize this overload and become frustrated when we fail to complete our regular duties. Without awareness, taking on too much can be unhealthy, unproductive, and unforgiving.

It is important to understand that regardless of what is challenging us in our lives, we create the bulk of our stress. I know this is hard for us to accept, but it is absolutely true. Our thoughts, how we perceive things, can substantially increase or decrease the amount of stress we experience. Events are neutral; it is our thinking that makes them good or bad.

To illustrate, let's pretend we are planning a big celebration. We can expect that no matter how carefully we prepare for that event, some problems will arise. Some challenges carry a greater potential for stress than others, but how well we deal with it still relates back to our thoughts on the subject.

Let's say we receive a call the day before the celebration informing us the caterer has cancelled. Here are some examples of thoughts a person might have upon hearing this news:

- This is terrible! The caterers can't cancel the day before the event. Everything is ruined!

- This is all my fault! I insisted on that caterer. Everyone will blame me.

- Okay, caterer has quit. Let's see who we can find to feed our hungry guests. There must be someone out there.

- Right on—a challenge! Let's see what we can do with this. Worst-case scenario, we make spaghetti and explain to anyone who complains.

Can you see how the different ways of thinking will affect the stress levels that accompany this problem? The first thought is going to result in increased stress and negativity. The second thought personalizes the problem, which adds guilt to the stress. The last two thoughts help us stay calm and deal with the situation, while the final idea has the added benefit of providing a positive spin and a fallback plan. To take things one step further, a person might decide this is an exciting opportunity to do something original and see it as incredibly good luck. So, while the caterer provided the challenge, our reaction (or thoughts), directly influenced the level of our stress.

What this boils down to is that we control our thoughts, and our thoughts greatly influence our stress. It makes sense to choose thoughts that help us feel calm and in control. When negative thoughts arise, it's in our best interest to quickly change our focus to something more positive. Developing a list of simple coping statements ("I can do this. Stay calm. Everything will work out") and then reaching for the feeling that comes with that thought, can keep things in perspective and remind us that we can handle whatever life throws our way.

Sometimes when faced with an intense situation, I take a step back and think about how significant, or insignificant, this will seem two years from now. In many cases, the current challenge, as awful as it seems, will clearly become no more than a humorous or at least thought-provoking story. If I'm still struggling to find the positives, I might take a moment and imagine how I would tell the story to a friend. When I do this, I naturally play up would-be funny parts forcing me to find the humor. Often what's most funny is my outrage and potential overreaction. People might think I've lost it when I start laughing in the middle of a crisis, but I'd rather they see me lose it to laughter then to a temper tantrum.

FREE Parenting Tip: Stress provides each of us with an opportunity to expand. Life is a journey and stress gives that journey purpose and direction. So, be the elastic. Get those boundaries in place so you don't overdo it, and then feel the stretch and enjoy.

Laughter is a great way to reduce stress, even if it starts out forced. When we have a real belly laugh we are releasing emotions that are pent up inside of us. Laughter is a wonderful way to release the tension that arises from stress. By becoming aware of the spots in our body where we hold tension, we can focus on relaxing those parts while we laugh.

This won't make the stressor disappear but will help us keep from snapping.

Sometimes this means that tears will join the laughter and, on occasion, we'll begin to cry. Letting tears out is a good thing, although it might be confusing at the moment. It is not helpful, however, if we allow the tears to take our thoughts into a negative zone ("Great, now I'm crying. It must be because of my dog Tobie dying. I'll never get over him. I miss him so much"). If we do this, the negative thoughts build tension, and we have undone whatever relief we had started to create.

Stress can also overwhelm us when we take on too much or try to be perfect at what we do. While we might not have total control over our workload, we can make it easier by allowing our work to be "good enough" rather than perfect. Pride in our work is an honorable quality to have, but not when perfectionism starts adding undue stress. There are many things we do (especially around the house) that do not need to be perfectly done. Often, when children enter our lives, we benefit by letting our standards relax a little.

It helps to take an honest look at our workload and determine where we can make changes to lighten things up. Often, there are people we never think to ask for help who would be more than willing to do so. By seeking out these people, we make connections and decrease the stress in our lives. We all need at least one good support in our life.

Finally, we need to be sure we aren't subscribing to that *never say no* attitude that makes us take on all kinds of things we don't want or need to be doing at that time. Knowing our limits and protecting them, helps us successfully deal with the important things. People will judge us more harshly for saying yes and failing to do a good job than for saying no in honor of our stress level.

Releasing the Pressure

Notice your internal critic. Any time you speak negatively to yourself replace the thought with something positive. For example, "Why am I always late?" becomes "I'm a few minutes late—tomorrow I'll leave earlier."

- Develop a list of coping statements. For example, "I can do this"; "Things always work out."

- Notice tension in your body and do stretches or exercises to work it out.

- Learn relaxation techniques for both mind and body.[29]

- Use laughter to reduce stress—even if it starts out forced.

- Separate your "to do" list into categories and then respond to them accordingly:

---

29   Meditation, yoga, and breathing exercises are all examples of relaxation techniques you might benefit from. There are many Web sites dedicated to these resources. One good one I have found is www.stress-relief-exercises. com.

❖ Things that *must* get done

For those things that must get done but still seem insurmountable, break them down into smaller steps. Asking for help when you need it is a sign of strength, so delegate wherever you can and then let it go.

❖ Things that *should* get done

These are often tasks like "washing the floor" and can be overlooked for a day or two. If you have a few that feel like really strong *shoulds,* assign them a priority number and deal with them only when the *musts* are fully looked after. You can also delegate these tasks whenever possible.

❖ Things that *would be nice* to get done but are not absolutely necessary

These are really bonus tasks and it's a good idea to remember that. If some of them are things you enjoy, put them in as a reward for getting a few items off your *must* list and then do them guilt-free.

❖ Things that *shouldn't* even be on the list

I'm not sure how these items get on our lists, but somehow they manage! Try boldly crossing them off, or writing beside them "Only when bored and all other tasks are completed." You could also try putting them in an envelope and mailing them (without a stamp) to the "Unnecessary Task Force." Once again, if you enjoy these items, keep them on there as rewards and use them for breaks from the more challenging jobs.

- Create a list of everything you can think of that causes you stress. You might need categories like: kids, partner, money, chores, and work. Go through the list and cross off or change any stressors outside of your control.

  For example, under the "work" category, you might have written "irritating colleague." You can't control his behaviour, so you could cross him off your list and remind yourself to ignore him, or revise it to "my reaction to irritating colleague," which puts it back under your control.

  Pick your three biggest stressors, or top one for each category, and develop a plan that might help you cope.
  Identify three positive qualities in this colleague every week. Take a course on how to work effectively with irritating people. Use him as data for a secret project and begin writing a book titled How Being Pleasant to Irritating People Affects Their Behaviour.

Little Things, Big Stress—A Look at Childcare

Although it might seem odd to focus on childcare in the self-care section of the book, this topic causes more stress for parents than almost any other. When our childcare is firmly and comfortably in place, we are calmer and have an easier time taking things in stride. When our childcare is unreliable, demanding, or concerning to us, our stress increases substantially. So while this topic might seem like one of the little things in our parenting world, it is one that can cause big stress and therefore well worth including in this section.

Finding good, quality people or organizations to care for our child and fit in our budget can be a challenge. This can be further complicated when we can't find a subsidized spot to put our child in. If we qualify for subsidized care, then going without is rarely an option. Even when good childcare has been found, we often still need help available for when our child is sick or our schedule has an unpredictable change.

I wish there was an easy answer I could give you for this. The truth is, you need reliable, flexible childcare that you can trust and feel good about in order to function well on a day to day basis. Additionally, if you do not work at a place that is understanding and supportive of your role as a parent, you will also suffer. Keep this in mind and be sure to ask those questions when deciding on work and childcare arrangements.

In our hearts, most of us recognize that parenting trumps all. When our kids are ill and need us, we need to be able to go to them. When our boss says that we cannot, the resentment, fear and frustration can be overwhelming. A good boss would recognize the quality of our work drops substantially when we are forced to stay.

Of course, we can have a great, understanding boss (we might even be the boss) but have something happening on a particular day that we simply can't get away from. This problem is even more frustrating when our child is not really ill but might be contagious (pink-eye, rashes, loose stool). How do we justify missing that important presentation or meeting when our child needs to go home (or to the doctor) just "in case" he has something?

Creating a support system you can count on is well worth the effort. Family, friends, neighbors, and other parents you meet at playgroups, etc., can all become part of this system. Strike up friendships whenever possible with other people who seem similar to you in needs and set up an exchange program ("If you help me out when I'm in a pinch, I will return the favour for you"). A good support system doesn't need to cost money if you can figure out a barter system that works for you both.

> FREE Parenting Tip: Having good childcare in place, along with a back-up plan, is going to make a big difference to your stress levels. Few of us like to ask for help, but when it comes to alternative childcare, sometimes we must.

You will want to be confident you can trust your childcare provider and be sure your kids are communicating to you about how they feel with that person or situation. There is a lot to be said for intuition, and, if something feels off, or your child seems uncomfortable around a person, it is worth further investigation. There are many great personal safety programs out there for young school-age children.[30] If your school is not teaching one, it's a good idea to access this information and teach it yourself. For very young children, you'll need to rely a lot on your instincts.

Many infants, toddlers, and preschoolers will cry when you drop them off because they would prefer to be with you. This should not be taken as a sign of bigger problems. Talk to the caregiver about what your child is like after you leave, and if you still have concerns pop in unpredictably to see for yourself. Even a phone call asking how she is doing and listening for her in the background can help to put your mind at ease. Throughout all of this, stay calm, focus on the positives, know that kids are very resilient, and listen to your gut.

---

30   Child Find (Kids in the Know) and Red Cross (RespectEd) offer two of the best programs where I live.

Our children are in our charge and most of us take that responsibility very seriously. The more alternatives we have to call on during times of need, the less stress we will experience. Having this *little thing* looked after in a way that allows us freedom and flexibility will make a big difference to our overall health.

Your Number-One Fan

How many times have you been there for someone when he or she was feeling down about life? Most of us do this quite naturally, not because we have to, but because we believe it's the right thing to do. The question becomes, how often do we do this for ourselves?

Most of us do an okay job of pointing out our successes and celebrating when things are going well. That's great, but it's not enough. A number-one fan is a person who believes in her hero even when his luck is down or he has made a substantial mistake. The fan doesn't dwell on mistakes or belittle her hero for taking a risk. This fan is there through thick and thin, cheering when things are going well and encouraging when things are not.

It's easy to be supportive when things are going well, but how many of us are able to keep smiling when things are not working out? Rather than being our number-one fan, many of us become the "fickle" fan and turn our back as soon as things go in a negative direction. We put ourselves down for making mistakes, point out each and every failing, and "should" all over ourselves. "I *should* have known better"; "I *should* work harder"; "I *should* go there right now." On occasion, we might even slip into self-pity: "Why me?"; "Why do things always go wrong for me?" And then feel worse when our memory digs deep and provides the answers.

The point is, while most of us try to be encouraging, many of us fall apart when the going gets tough. We've been taught to do this, and it's an extremely tough pattern to break. We need to practice not just liking ourselves but actually being our number-one fan.

Self-care, taking the time to recharge our batteries and keep ourselves in top form, is one important way to do this. This means taking time out of our busy schedules to focus on our own rest and relaxation. It's about believing that we are truly deserving of such a thing—guilt-free! This is not about doing things with or for our kids because it feels good and we like to do it (for example, reading a bedtime story), but about really focusing on the things we need as an individual to keep our batteries charged.

For example, if you love to run and used to do it all the time before having your child, what can you do now to build that back into your life? Running around playing does not create the same self-care connection. So play with your child and enjoy it, but put equal effort and creativity into fitting a well-deserved run into your schedule.

Sometimes people adopt a healthier self-care focus after experiencing a life-threatening illness or major life transition (divorce, job loss, significant death). It is sad that a major threat is required to shift our way of thinking, but for many people that is what it takes.

To be at the top of our game, we have to pay attention to our own needs before focusing on those around us. On an airplane, when they give the lifesaving instructions at the start of the flight, they will always remind us to put on our own oxygen mask before trying to assist others, even our children. They do this because if we are unconscious (or dead) due to lack of oxygen, we aren't going to be much help to anyone else.

The message we get from this can be applied in every area of our lives. We will be the greatest help to others when we look after ourselves first.

Examples of self-care include: alone time, bathing, reading, drawing, yoga, walking, chatting, running. There is no right or wrong when it comes to self-care, unless you never participate in it. A number-one fan would go out of her way to encourage her hero to look after herself. Since you are the fan *and* the hero, do what you must to make sure self-care happens.

If that's not enough to make you sit down and create of list of things to do for yourself, then I have one more piece of wisdom to share. The way we feel about ourselves, how secure we are, how worthy we feel, how tuned in we are, how much self-care we practice, are all picked up by the people around us. Our kids are affected by how good (or bad) we feel. We help them by helping ourselves first.

Practice makes perfect, and this is the kind of perfect I believe we should all strive to reach. So pick a minimum twenty minutes each day and put yourself first. Raise those pom-poms and start teaching your kids how to be a number-one fan.

> *FREE Parenting Tip: Often parents get so caught up helping their children be happy, they forget to schedule in any time for themselves. The things you do to keep yourself strong and functioning at the top of your game directly influences your child's ability to do the same.*

Exercise: Bag It All!

This exercise is a visualization that can be used to reduce stress or declutter your brain. Read it through, and then sit back, close your eyes, and watch it happen.

Take a couple of deep, cleansing breaths while picturing a beautiful bag. The bag is rich in colour, soft in texture, and strong in structure. It has a drawstring at the top allowing you to stick your fingers in and pull it wide open.

Take a moment and reflect on the things that are currently causing you stress. As each one comes to mind, pull it out and put it in the bag. You might want to work in categories like health issues, family concerns, work challenges, weather situations, money woes, and so on. Don't worry about overfilling the bag; it can hold unlimited amounts of stress. Continue to work through your mind until your stresses have all been put into the bag.

When you are done, take a moment and notice any places in your body where you still feel tension. Try breathing into that spot, and, when you exhale, blow the tension out with your breath. If a new stress comes to mind, pull it out and add it to your collection.

When you are done removing stresses, pull the drawstring tight, wrap it around the neck of the bag a few times, and finish it with a knot. Gently put the bag away in a spot in your mind that feels safe, like on a shelf, under a chair, or in a cave.

Take a deep cleansing breath and open your eyes. Throughout the day, when a worry tries to surface, cut it off with a positive thought like "Today, I am stress-free."

New stresses arise very quickly in our lives, so revisit the bag as often as you wish, and for now just enjoy your stress break.

Exercise Alternatives

Although visualization exercises are a tool well worth working to achieve, if you find they add stress instead of removing it, try one of following options instead.

- Draw a bag on a piece of paper and then follow through the exercise by writing words or creating images to represent your stressors inside the bag. Be sure to do the breathing and tension-removing pieces as you do your drawing.

- Find a nice bag and collect small objects you can use to represent your stresses as well as small slips of paper. As you work through the exercise, deposit objects or write your stressors on slips of paper to put in the bag. Do not rush the process and do not omit the breathing and tension-releasing or you might find your deep-seated stressors will stay buried and tension will not leave your body.

Because these exercises give you something more concrete to work with, I would suggest you dump the bag out at the end of each day into a tub and/or destroy the papers. Reading them will only bring your stressors back into your conscience, so this is not a picture you want to post up or dwell on in any way throughout your day. The idea is to release the pent-up tension that comes from holding on to these thoughts. Once they have been moved from your mind to the bag, the objects have done their job and are no longer important.

Chapter 13: Keeping a Healthy Perspective

My Extracurricular Challenge

My daughter was never into extracurricular activities although we always encouraged her to participate. Over a span of six years, we offered her a variety of options: Toddler Play Gym, Music for Young Children, swimming, Scouts—all without pressure to join and never taking more than one at a time. Despite this, in every situation she would ask to sign up, get nervous about attending, go to the first couple sessions, and then decide she wanted to quit. Commitment is very important in our family, and, since we'd already discussed this prior to joining, we insisted she finish each program. It was exhausting to get her there and nearly impossible to gain her participation. No matter how patient I was when I started out each week, almost every occasion ended in tears.

Imagine our surprise when our daughter decided she should sign up for kung fu with her brother. It would be in a gym environment filled with many sweaty kids kicking and making loud noises. She dislikes crowds, new environments, noisy situations, and being the center of attention.[31] The chances of her actually completing the program were small, so we did extra talking about what this commitment would mean. She insisted she wanted to do this, and, since she was now nine (a couple years older than she was during the last struggle), we signed her up.

My husband was in charge of taking both kids to kung fu the first evening and arrived home looking very unhappy. When I asked what had happened, he told me our daughter had decided not to participate and there was nothing he could do to gain her compliance.

At first I was furious. A piece of me wanted to teach her a lesson she would never forget. We had spent so much time preparing so this would not happen, and now we were faced with seven weeks of battling to get her out the door. Worse yet, the chances of her participating after sitting out the first session were pretty much zero.

Realizing anger would not help, I told my daughter that her dad and I needed time to decide what to do about this and that it wouldn't hurt for her to give some thought to possible consequences as well. I racked my brain to come up with a solution, but nothing came. My husband and I talked about it, and only three things came to mind:

---

31 *The Highly Sensitive Child* by **Elaine Aron is a fantastic book that helped me to understand my daughter better and to recognize things about myself that I had never understood before.**

1. She could not be allowed to just quit.

2. Neither of us had the energy to force her to go.

3. Struggling with her every week to get her there would not be fair to our son.

The next day, I sat down with my daughter and told her we needed to brainstorm ways to solve this problem. Our solution needed to have a strong learning component for her, and it needed to deal with the loss of the course fee. Picking up a paper and pen, I got ready to write.

Identify problem: Alissa was signed up in a program she no longer wished to attend, but had promised to complete.

Develop list of solutions (brainstorm):

*   I suggested Alissa could be strong and force herself to participate and finish the program.

*   Alissa rallied and said she could go live with Grandma.

*   I suggested we could kidnap her instructor and lock him up so the program could not run. I needed to decrease the rising tension in the room and get us thinking creatively.

*   Alissa offered to pay for the course out of her allowance and not be allowed to sign up for another program for one year, which showed me that she had been giving this some serious thought!

*   Alissa added the idea that she could clean her room weekly, a big undertaking that I would not have thought was relevant.

- Alissa's dad suggested we could fly Jackie Chan to our house to provide private kung fu lessons (an idea he shared just to prove he could be goofier than me).

- Alissa suggested we ask our son's friend if he would like to take her spot for a discounted price, making both her father and me wonder at her obvious maturity.

- Alissa offered to attend and watch the program each week but not participate.

Our "goofy" solutions were quickly crossed off the list as unrealistic, illegal, or too expensive. Alissa developed the final solution herself by making a creative blend of a few of them.

Evaluate solutions and choose what to use: Alissa would phone the mother of our son's friend, explain the situation, and see if her son wanted to attend kung fu in her place for a discounted price. Alissa would cover the difference (from her allowance), would attend and watch each session, and would clean her room weekly for the duration of the program.

Assess how it worked: That evening Alissa phoned and set it up for the other child to take her spot. She contracted to pay us the twenty-dollar difference over five months and, with my husband's help, explained the situation to the teacher. She attended every session without complaint and cleaned her room weekly.

Since then, Alissa has participated in a few programs (drawing class, sewing, badminton) but has explained to me many times that she prefers unstructured activities. Without any instruction, she dances at home and sings constantly. When possible, we take her to free-skating and play on the ice in our yard. She swims at our cabin and fills her spare time with writing, drawing, painting, reading, and crafting. She succeeds at almost everything she tries and does it at her own pace, using her own unique style. She did a good job at solving this problem, and I was very happy I let her.

What Do We Need?

Time and energy are much-sought-after commodities in our fast-paced world. For many of us, the pressure to provide our children with lots of opportunities can be very intense. We enroll them in every program we think will be beneficial to their development and then run around trying to get them to these important learning experiences. This pressure increases when we have more than one child, particularly if we're a single parent.

As a result, the years when our kids are growing up can become a blur of fast food, schedule-juggling, bossy parenting, and rushing around. These programs can be expensive, especially when they involve out-of-town events. Financial stress can add to the pressure, yet a parent offered extra work is in an even greater bind. Frustration, guilt, and resentment are common in these situations.

It is wonderful to encourage our kids to participate in extra activities; however, we need to keep the big picture in mind. As with most things in life, there needs to be a balance. Here are a few reasons we might want to make changes:

1. Putting a child into many programs can create a lot of stress for our kids. Children need some downtime to process what they have learned. They need opportunities to do nothing and learn

how to enjoy themselves while doing it. In fact, that is part of their self-care. Having some structure in their lives is healthy; having every day structured is not.

2. While our world might revolve around our child, it is not our intention to make him think he is the center of everyone's universe. It is great for him to look out for number one—that is a healthy perspective. It is not okay for him to expect everyone else to do this as well. In fact, we can't model being our number-one fan and dedicate all our time to our child's schedule.

3. Kids thrive on some routine. When we put our children into a number of different things, the routine might seem similar (rush from school, eat quickly, and get out the door), but it is still quite different. Having soccer one night, guitar the next, then Scouts on the third requires a lot of mental shifting and can result in acting out.

How do we focus on our own personal development and still be a good parent? We do this by taking a look at family activities and commitments, including the extracurricular items, and separating them into categories of *needs* versus *wants*. *Needs* are the things we must do to survive, while *wants* are the things we would like to do.

We would likely agree that to survive we need access to food and water. For many, that translates into a need for money, which further indicates a need for income. What's important to keep in mind is that only you can determine the difference between what you need and what you want. Those things we decide we cannot live without become our needs, while all other things are wants. If you are the kind of person who can justify anything, this might be challenging for you to take an honest look at.

Perhaps the easiest way to do this is to take those things identified as important and rate them on a scale from one to ten with ten being really important to you. Things rated at eight and higher should always be seriously considered, but be careful not to score everything in that range.

Recognize that there are many different ways to satisfy a need. For example, if a doctor told me my son needs to be in hockey to work off his high energy, I might think hockey is a need. What she really meant was that my son needs some kind of regular activity to burn off his high energy. That opens the door to many organized sports as well as unstructured activities. Putting him in hockey would not be wrong, but it's good to have options. In this case, hockey might satisfy both a need and a want. If I put my son in hockey, but he didn't want to play, it would qualify as a need only.

Remember that *wants* are things we will always have and will never be able to totally satisfy. It's good to want things; they provide us with goals to work toward. It's when we believe we are entitled to our every want being fulfilled and punish others when they are not that we have a problem.

Finally, it's wonderful to have supports and allow ourselves to use them to make things work in our families. If there are wants we really would like our kids to be able to satisfy, then figuring out ways to get them to these opportunities (like a carpool) works in our favour. Using a shared driving system might mean missing some events, but when it allows an involvement that might not otherwise be possible, it's a great option to have.

As long as we are striving to be part of our kids' lives and taking an interest in their activities, we need not worry about always being able to go. Special events (for example, our child's winter concert) might interfere with our regular commitment (volunteering or swimming lessons), but recognizing that our presence at these events makes a difference to our kids is important. Juggling our schedule to be there shows our kids their achievements matter to us even when we have other things on the go. It really is all about balance.

By understanding the difference between needs and wants, we can become aware of how balanced things are in our families and then make necessary changes. Remember, you are the expert in your family. If your kids are in numerous activities and the family is happy doing things that way, keep up the great work. If your child seems destined to be a future star in an activity and you want to take every opportunity to make that happen, go for it. Just be aware of the happiness level versus the amount of stress involved and be sure to aim for balance.

> *FREE Parenting Tip: Trying to please everyone in our family can create stress, guilt, and anxiety. By recognizing the difference between needs and wants, we can set priorities that work for everyone. Our health and happiness might depend on it.*

Putting Our Needs First

Putting your life into categories can be as challenging as getting balanced in the first place. You know your family and life situation better than anyone else. Only you can determine the needs and wants within that structure. What's important is that you are honest with yourself and open to the idea of making changes where necessary. Use your inner voice to guide you. You'll know when things need fixing.

Once you understand the difference between needs and wants you can use this information to help balance things out in your home life. Use the following points to guide you in this process:

- Create a list of all the activities each person in your household participates in. Look at required commitments (school, work, homework) as well as programs (soccer, music, Scouts) and regular requests (play dates, library, family outings). Do not list anything occasional, for example an evening of swimming for a birthday party would not make the list, but regular swimming lessons or swimming weekly at free swim would.

- Put an N (need) or W (want) beside each of the things listed. Note: If a parent is making a child take something (for example, piano), put it as a *need*. If your child asked to sign up, even if later that season she wanted to quit, list it as a *want*. Use your family values to help you identify definite needs (homework, church, volunteering).

- Create a table with each person's name down the side and the days of the week across the top. Fill in the grid with the *needs* listed first. Once they are in place start adding in the *wants*.

- Take an objective look at the chart. Is it balanced? Is one person allowed to satisfy numerous *wants* while another is meeting only *needs*? It's fair to limit the number of *wants* for your child, especially if his *want* is taking up more than one day of the week.

Looking at the Sample Family Chart, the family identified its needs as school, work, church, and volunteering, which are listed at the top of each person's row because they are priorities. Homework is also a priority, but because the kids always get it done when required, the family did not list it as "dedicated" time. Each family member has a first *want* and the son a second *want*.

After creating this chart and using it to structure their weekly activities, the son requested an after-school sport on Wednesdays, but was told that unless he could arrange the rides, he could not, as that would interfere with both dad's and sister's first *wants*. If it had been on Thursdays, the family might have agreed, but not unless they were sure it didn't conflict with a second *want* for anyone else or be too much for any of them to handle.

When one person does a lot of one or two-day events, these won't show on the chart but could be included in the picture. For example, because I work mostly out of our house, I try to make a point of getting out regularly. I volunteer twice a month, so for the other weeks I try to plan an outing with a friend or participate in a workshop. To accommodate this in my chart, I write the word *out* in the *want* column on Tuesdays and Thursdays. Everyone knows these are flexible, and I don't let it interfere with any scheduled events.

In families in which parents work shifts, travel a lot, or are parenting alone, you might need to be really creative in how to set up your chart.

Sample Family Chart

	N/W	Sat	Sun	Mon	Tues	Wed	Thurs	Fri
Mom	Needs		Work	Work		Work (eve)		
	Wants	Yoga					Volunteer	
Dad	Needs		Church	Work	Work	Work	Work	Work
	Wants					Curling	Volunteer	
Sue	Needs		Church	School	School	School	School	School
	Wants	Volleyball				Volleyball		
Max	Needs		Church	School	School	School	School	School
	Wants	Soccer		Soccer	Music			Soccer

Having a few people you can count on to watch a sibling or drive your kids can help decrease the stress of making those last-minute arrangements.

As our kids become more independent and no longer require us to drive them everywhere, the chart may become obsolete. The only caution with this is that sometimes newfound freedom will cause a family to fan out into their personal interests and forget to do anything together. Over time, this weakens relationships, so be aware and perhaps keep a family gathering or two on the list of needs.

Where Does All Our Time Go?

If we were provided with a monthly chart of what is taking up our time and energy, we would probably be shocked at the results. In real life, things have a way of sneaking up on us, taking up a lot of our time, and then becoming important because they take up so much time. Countless amounts of energy can get lost in doing things we don't enjoy or would consider unimportant, and then we wonder why we can't seem to get everything done. Life has a way of taking over and running itself if we don't put ourselves firmly in the driver's seat.[32]

It is important that we find balance in our lives. If we invest all our time in making money so our children can lead happy lives, but invest no time in our children, we are missing the big picture. If we put all our time into advancing our career and then get downsized out of a job, our identity is in danger of going with it. There is no award for the cleanest

---

32   *First Things First* **by Stephen Covey and Rebecca and Roger Merrill is an excellent read on this topic.**

house and investing lots of time watching life on a screen instead of living it won't provide a lot of life satisfaction.

> *FREE Parenting Tip: Time and energy can get used up on trivial tasks if you aren't paying attention. Take a moment to figure out your current picture and ensure you are putting your time and energy into things that are truly important to you.*

Many people find out what's truly important to them when it's too late to turn back and do much about it. By asking ourselves "Where does all my time go?" and taking a moment to figure out the answer, we are putting ourselves firmly in the driver's seat, before reaching the point of no return.

Exercise: Creating Your Picture

There are two strategies I find useful for helping people figure out how they spend their time—one for those who like to play with numbers and one for everybody else. Use whichever style you like better or choose a different one altogether. Just do your best to become aware of how your time is spent. Read through and decide which one suits your needs better rather than doing both.

Strategy #1: Giving One Hundred Percent

Monthly Activity Sample Chart

volunteer	gardener	banker
hockey parent	housecleaner	yard worker
yoga	runner	daughter
internet surfer	swimmer	mother
photographer	employee	sister
reader	stamp collector	husband
baker/chef	musician	son

Brainstorm everything you do on a monthly basis (see Monthly Activity Sample Chart) and then start fitting the different items into categories (for example, running, Pilates and badminton could all be put under "exercise"). If possible limit your number of categories to nine. You're going to be creating a grid that looks something like Activity Grid #1.

Activity Grid #1

Part-time employee	Dog owner	Mother/wife
Daughter/sister	Exercise	Friend
Self-care	Self-employed	Other: Housework

Once you've created categories, try to determine the percentage of time per month you spend in each area. For example, I walk my dog for an hour twice a day. Every once in a while, I delegate the evening or weekend walk to someone else, so total time probably equals forty hours per month. Since I'm awake about sixteen hours a day (using a thirty-day month), I list dog owner as using twelve percent of my time.

$$(30 \times 16) = 480 \div 40 \text{ hrs} = 12\%$$

I could include eleven percent under exercise and one percent in household chores for feeding/letting her in and out, etc. This varies depending on the month but this is the typical picture. If something happens and I'm suddenly spending a lot more time with my dog (for example, taking her to training), my grid tells me I cannot do that without decreasing my time and energy somewhere else.

For some people, it will work easier to take the first month to determine their grid. Write down everything you do the first day and approximate amount of time you spend doing it. The next day, add anything new to your list along with any major adjustments in time. Continue to do this until you feel ready to generalize the information to create a one-month picture.

This will help you identify problem areas in which time and energy are being used unnecessarily and provide you with an idea of how much time you can afford to dedicate to any one category. Be careful not to make this logging activity another drain on your time! The numbers are what create the picture, but don't get so caught up in them that you can't finish your grid. Try to make it a fair reflection of your current life that totals one hundred.

Using a scale of one to ten with ten being extremely important, think about how important each category is to you and assign it a number. Once you've rated them, put a star beside those categories that make you feel stronger and an X in any that drain your energy. Some categories will both strengthen and weaken you as demonstrated in Activity Grid #2.

Activity Grid #2

Part-time employee	Dog owner	Mother/wife
5% - 2 - *	12% - 7 - *	20% - 10 - */x
Daughter/sister	Exercise	Friend
2% - 8 - */x	3% - 6 - *	8% - 8 - *
Self-care	Self-employed	Other: Housework
15% - 9 - *	25% - 10 - *	10% - 3 – x

It's totally up to you how you categorize things and how much you break them down. What's important is that you keep the grid small enough to be workable but detailed enough to guide you.

Use the grid to study your picture. Putting a lot of time into housework probably isn't a good idea if it's a low priority and weakens you. Perhaps you need to hire a housecleaner, or make sure the chores are shared with your family. If this is not possible, you might need to lower your standards of how tidy the house looks. Ask yourself what's more important, a spotless house or happiness and see if you can find that balance?

On the other hand, if you enjoy housework (some people claim they find it therapeutic!), you might consider offering to do some cleaning for your neighbor in exchange for emergency childcare time or walking your dog once a week. Look for those things you rate low or draining versus those you rate high or energizing to see if you can create a minimum of twice as many energizing than draining categories.

This grid can also help you become aware of possible problems on the rise. For example, if you aren't putting any time into self-care but a lot into a draining job, you could be headed for burnout. By the same token, if the bulk of your time is spent at work, with the rest focused on jobs at home (cleaning, maintenance, etc.), you might find you're too depleted to ever feel happy. At least one of those things would have to be an energizer for you to keep going.

We cannot give more than one hundred percent of our time. When we add something new into our lives, we must be willing to give up time and energy from somewhere else. We can steal from less important categories, like television time, but be careful not to take from critical areas like sleep and self-care, or the new activity will not be worth it in the end.

Strategy #2: What's on Your Plate?

Another way to do this exercise is to draw a circle on a piece of paper. This is your plate. Write down everything you are responsible for doing in a week or month. Underline or highlight those you enjoy and then circle (or highlight with a different colour) those you would like to spend less time doing. You might even use a third highlighter to indicate those things you really dislike doing and a fourth for those you really wish you could spend more time at.

Write down anything that's not on your plate but that you wish you had time to do around the outside of your circle. Give some thought to how you might remove some of the "dislikes" or change them to find more enjoyment in them. For example, walking my dog twice a day started to become a burden about six months into the task. I realized that to make it fun again I needed to do something different. I started recording teleseminars and then listening to them while I walked. It made the walks enjoyable again and helped me keep up this activity I see as important.

Sometimes it works to break down things that seem unattainable into smaller steps to see if you can add just one little piece of it into your world. Ideally, our goal would be to have twice as many things in the *like* category as in the *dislike* category.

Conclusion

Our dilemma is that we hate change and love it at the same time; what we really want is for things to remain the same but get better.

— Sydney J. Harris

Embracing Change

Changing the way we parent is not an easy task. When things are familiar, they feel comfortable to us, even when we know they don't work. When we try something new, we are taking a risk and opening ourselves up for possible failure. New things feel awkward, adding to our discomfort and providing a reason for avoiding them. With time and practice, these problems disappear; the awkwardness goes away, and we become comfortable with our new way of doing things.

Unfortunately, many of us give up change in the awkward phase. We write things off before we get used to them and decide our kids are "too bad for that tool." Sometimes we'll decide our child's problem behaviour is no big deal and not worth the effort to change. If our kids resist the change and their behaviour gets worse before it gets better (which should be expected), not only do we write off the new tool, we also label the tool as the problem. In other words, rather than push ourselves through the awkwardness of change, we allow the discomfort to stop our progress and increase our resistance to changing.

Life is like that. The things that are really worthwhile take effort on our part. Building character and relationships with our kids are not small jobs and will require many adjustments along the way. Helping our kids grow into resilient, resourceful, human beings is a journey requiring patience and confidence in our ability. It's well worth the effort, but definitely not easy.

People will embrace change once they have decided it is necessary to do so. If others are pushing them to change, even with the best of intentions, they will fight it tooth and nail. Our energy would be better spent focused on our own areas of growth.

Many of us resist change because it means we have to modify learned behaviours. If you've put eight years into parenting, it is going to be a lot harder to change your patterns than it would be if you are starting with a newborn.

Resistance to change is also what keeps us focused and on task. If we didn't resist change at all, we'd never get anywhere. Most of us have met people who can't make up their mind and change their plans more often then they keep them. While this might work for them, most of us would rather be more decisive.

As a species we will not change unless we believe it is essential to do so. If we can take advantage of the good moments in our parenting life and work in baby steps to make positive changes, we can make it through the awkwardness and begin to reap the rewards. Embracing the change means accepting that as we learn we grow and as we grow we learn.

> *FREE Parenting Tip: Change is a process that takes time and determination, so be kind to yourself.*

Breaking Free

Parenting will always be a bit of a mystery. Who knows why some parenting ideas work and others do not? Or why some kids seem to succeed despite family setbacks, while others have so much given to them and yet fail to thrive? The one thing we do know is that once you have a child you'll never be quite the same again. Awe-inspiring emotions like overwhelming love, extreme guilt, intense frustration, and incredible joy make this job second to none.

Breaking free of parenting pressures means recognizing the pieces that make us unique, the pieces that we carry with us from the past, and the pieces that are influenced by the society we live in. When we can pick and choose which pieces we want to keep around and change the others to align with our inner wisdom, we will feel more self-assured in our role as a parent.

Although it is challenging, parenting is the way we will leave a mark on our world. Let's leave it with confidence!

About the Author

Debbie is a parent educator, speaker, and workshop leader. She is a mother of two who believes all parents can benefit from support and encouragement at some point in their parenting journey. She lives on a small acreage in Manitoba, Canada with her husband, two teenagers, and numerous pets.

Bibliography

Chapman, Gary. *The Five Love Languages: How to Express Heartfelt Commitment to Your Mate.* Chicago, IL: Northfield Publishing, 2004.

Coloroso, Barbara. *Kids Are Worth It! Giving Your Child the Gift of Inner Discipline.* Toronto, ON: Somerville House, 1995.

Covey, Stephen. *The 7 Habits of Highly Effective Families.* New York: Golden Books, 1997.

Faber, Adele and Elaine Mazlish. *How to Talk So Kids Will Listen and Listen So Kids Will Talk.* New York: Avon Books, 1980.

Gossen, Diane Chelsom. *My Child is a Pleasure.* Saskatoon, SK: Chelsom Consultants Limited, 1997.

Lipton, Bruce. H., *The Wisdom of Your Cells: How Your Beliefs Control Your Biology.* Sounds True Audio Learning, 2007.

Potter-Efron, Ron. *Angry All the Time: An Emergency Guide to Anger Control.* Oakland, CA: New Harbinger, 1994.

Sanders, Matthew. *Triple P Select Practitioner Manual, University of Queensland,* 2004

Robbins, Anthony. *Personal Power II.* San Diego, CA: Robbins Research International, 1996.

Resources

Further Reading

Aron, Elaine N. *The Highly Sensitive Child: Helping Our Children Thrive When the World Overwhelms Them.* New York: Broadway Books, 2002.

Covey, Sean. *The 6 Most Important Decisions You'll Ever Make: A Guide for Teens.* New York: Simon & Schuster, 2006.

Covey, Stephen, R., A. Roger Merrill & Rebecca R. Merrill. *First Things First.* Provo, UT: Covey Leadership Center, 1994.

Goleman, Daniel. *Emotional Intelligence: Why It Can Matter More Than IQ.* New York: Bantam Books, 1994.

Gray, John. *Men Are From Mars, Women Are From Venus.* New York: HarperCollins Publishers, 1993.

Hicks, Jerry & Esther. *The Astonishing Power of Emotions: Let Your Feelings Be Your Guide.* Carlsbad, CA: Hay House, 2007.

Horn, Sam. *Tongue Fu! How to Deflect, Disarm and Defuse Any Verbal Conflict.* New York: St. Martins Press, 1996.

Jackson, Adam J. *The Ten Secrets of Abundant Happiness: Simple Lessons for Creating the Life You Want.* New York: Harper Paperbacks, 1996.

Nelsen, Jane. *Positive Discipline.* Toronto, ON: Random House of Canada, 1996.

Phelan, Thomas. W. *1-2-3 Magic: Effective Discipline for Children 2 -12.* Glen Ellyn, Illinois: Child Management Inc., 1995.

Reigh, Maggie. *9 Ways to Bring Out the Best in You and Your Child.* Kelowna, BC: Northstone Publishing, 2004.

Robbins, Anthony. *Awaken the Giant Within: How to Take Immediate Control of Your Mental, Emotional, Physical and Financial Destiny.* New York: Simon & Schuster, 1991.

Tracy, Brian. *Maximum Achievement: Strategies and Skills That Will Unlock Your Hidden Powers to Succeed.* New York: Simon & Schuster, 1993.

Web Sites

The author's Web Site http://www.empoweringnrg.com offers many other articles on related topics, links to her social networking sites, along with contact information for bookings.

This Web Site http://www.bullies2buddies.com provides great information for how to truly help your child with the concerning topic of bullying.